How to HAVE FUN —*without*— GETTING *into* TROUBLE

How to HAVE FUN — *without* — GETTING *into* TROUBLE

Simcha Feuerman
& Chaya Feuerman

JASON ARONSON INC.
Northvale, New Jersey
Jerusalem

]

This book is dedicated to our parents, rebbeim, and teachers
who have provided us with
education, guidance, and love.

Library of Congress Cataloguing-in-Publication Data

Feuerman, Simcha, 1967–
    How to have fun without getting into trouble / Simcha and Chaya Feuerman
        p. cm.
    Includes index.
    ISBN 0-7657-6174-2
    1. Interpersonal relations—Religious aspects—Judaism. 2. Interpersonal relations.
3. Parent and child—Religious aspects—Judaism. 4. Parent and child—
Psychological aspects. 5. Self-actualization (Psychology)—Religious aspects
Judaism. 6. Self-actualization (Psychology) I. Feuerman, Chaya, 1968- II. Title.

    BM723 F.44 2002
    296.7—dc21   00–061061

Acknowledgments

We offer thanks to the Almighty for providing us with the great traditions of the Torah and our very humanity, allowing us to explore the wonders of creation.

We also give special thanks to our dear brother and brother-in-law, Yisrael Feuerman, who thought of the clever title for this book which, after all, is about what many religious people are trying to find out: "How to have fun without getting into trouble!"

The thoughts in this book are based on our weekly column in the Family Pages of the Jewish Press. We thank the editors and staff of the Jewish Press for all their help over the years, particularly Naomi Mauer and Sheila Abrams.

Table of Contents

Part Three: The Self

Introduction

As psychotherapists, we have encountered many religious Jews today who report that they feel pulled in different directions. They have a love and respect for the traditions of the Torah, but have also absorbed and benefited from many of the secular and Western values of the modern world.

As a result of these tensions, many religious Jews have made uneasy compromises leading to a patchwork of conflicting personal values and philosophies. We have found that this contributes to a sense of guilt, anger, and confusion. Below are some examples of the social, psychological, and religious dilemmas facing religious Jews today:

- A husband and wife have serious disagreements over matters of religion.
- A young woman is feeling tormented about doubts she has in matters of faith.
- Parents cannot seem to get their child to behave properly in shul.
- A teenager who has spent a year studying in Israel does not want to return home. Instead, he wants to stay and continue learning Torah. The parents believe he should pursue a secular career, but his teachers have advised him

that he does not need to listen to them, as they are corrupted by American and materialistic values.

- An observant and committed Jew wonders if the same Torah that prohibits jealousy and commands one to "Love your neighbor" allows for an individual to express his or her feelings, or if feelings must be controlled, repressed, and "bottled up." If so, is this emotionally healthy?
- A family wonders how they can, as Americans and religious Jews, make peace with the materialism and opulence that surrounds them. The parents wonder how they can teach their children core values in a world and society that seem to disregard and disrespect the sacred.
- An accomplished and mature adult is having difficulty with his parents. He wonders, "How can I harmonize the American values of independence, self-determination, and freedom of speech with the apparently restrictive rules of the Torah? Can a mature and self-respecting man of the twenty-first century follow the strict traditional requirements of 'Honor thy father and thy mother?' "
- A young man or young woman wonders how to approach dating and relationships. Is true love the most important requirement? What is the Torah philosophy? Is it in conflict with what people consider emotionally stable and healthy behavior?
- Parents of a growing family, with many small children, are feeling overwhelmed. How do they manage the financial pressures of modern Jewish life? How can the schools expect them to earn enough money to pay for the tuition, *and* be home to supervise each child's two hours' worth of homework each night? Is there parenting advice out there for people who have more than "the American ideal of 1.2 children?"
- A committed and deeply religious Jew has been experiencing emotional problems. His family and doctor have recommended that he see a psychotherapist. He won-

ders why the Torah and *mussar* books (Jewish inspirational and ethical teachings) are not sufficient to help a person improve himself?

From whom should the above questioners seek counsel? A rabbi? A psychotherapist? What are the similarities and differences between rabbinic advice or *mussar* and psychotherapeutic treatment, and how does one decide which is the best route to solve his or her problem? To answer this question properly, we must clarify the goals and operating principles of each discipline.

The rabbi serves as a representative of the Torah, and provides advice on how to live life successfully. This stems from a religious belief that the Torah is meant as a guidebook for how humans ought to act and behave. Though there are many aspects of the Torah that one can experience as personally beneficial and enjoyable, the Torah perspective does not consider personal happiness *in this world* as an ultimate goal, as it teaches that there will be a final reckoning in the world to come. (See the first chapter of the *Mesilas Yesharim*, by Rabbi Moshe Chaim Luzzatto.) If a religious person is able to follow the advice and guidelines of the Torah, and is able to use them to overcome personal and emotional difficulties, some may legitimately argue that he will have little use for a psychotherapist. However, others may find that despite their efforts to improve their character through the study of *mussar* and other religious advice, they cannot manage to resolve certain personal problems. Such problems may be in the area of personal emotions, for example, depression or lack of self-confidence, or in marital and familial relationships.

A therapist operates from a different perspective than a rabbi. There is a popular misconception that a good therapist gives good advice to patients. Actually, a good therapist should not be giving *any* advice. The goal of psychotherapy is, as the saying goes, "to teach people *how* to fish instead of giving them fish." If you think about this for a moment, you will realize that most people experiencing emotional difficulties already have legions of friends and relatives giving them advice and telling them what to do. Even strangers volunteer with unsolicited advice. A therapist's job is to help the person find his own way and learn how to make the most helpful choices for himself. This may sound simple, but it actually takes years of training, experience, and a good deal of natural talent. To provide this form of help, one must be able to master two opposite and conflicting skills. On one hand, the therapist must join the patient emotionally and try to understand the situation completely from the patient's perspective. On the other hand, the therapist must be able to stay detached enough from the problem to help the patient begin to see his situation with objective and neutral eyes. A therapist endeavors to help a person fully understand what personal feelings and choices contribute to his or her current difficulties and what other possible feelings, cognitions, actions, and choices are available that may be more helpful. A therapist is less concerned with what is right or wrong morally than he is concerned with what is preventing his patient from accomplishing whatever goals he sets. In other words, *mussar* tries to teach a person the "right way" to think and act. Psychotherapy, instead of trying to change a person, tries to help one understand how and why he is currently thinking and acting a certain way. Both of these approaches can ultimately affect a change, but they accomplish them through different means. *Mussar* dictates morals and advice directly, while psychotherapy attempts to assist a person in learning more about himself, which can help a person change if he so chooses.

After the above definitions, you might wonder what the point is in psychotherapy, if all it does is help people understand their situation better. Actually, many people who have had a true and professionally executed psychotherapeutic process find it extremely valuable and helpful. This is because, as we have alluded to before, most people experiencing difficulties get way too much advice, and comparatively little patience, understanding, and respect. After all, who has the patience to sit with someone, listen to him whine, and even lend encouragement for him to work through the possible choices and solutions *without* trying to force him to follow this or that advice? A really good friend may be able to do this for an hour or so. But a therapist is trained and paid to do this for an extended period of time. Since people change slowly, those who want to help a person change must be able to be patient and work slowly.

An additional point to consider is that often people are not fully aware of their underlying feelings and emotions. Without examining them more closely, and without having the benefit of a person who is trained to see certain patterns of human behavior and internal defense mechanisms that people construct, it is not always possible to get to the heart of a problem. Many psychological theories ascribe to the idea that the mind is working on different levels and some decisions may have unconscious motivations that cannot be dealt with unless a person becomes more aware of them. For example, a person may come for treatment because he frequently loses his job due to his getting into fights and power struggles with supervisors. His spouse or parents have given him plenty of "advice," such as, "Why do you have to argue so much? Why are you looking for fights? Get a new job before you quit your present one, if you are unhappy!"

One may wonder, why is this advice not working? Presumably, it is because some underlying condition is contributing to the problem and blocking this person from making more practical judgments. That is the work of the therapy to uncover and hopefully allow the person a more constructive way to deal with the issue. For example, perhaps the patient has some career goal that he is afraid to follow but is constantly restless in his current job. Is there a more realistic and constructive way to pursue this goal? Or maybe this patient sees his boss as too important in his life and looks for compliments and self-esteem from his boss. When he gets criticism instead of praise, he reacts in an unconstructive manner more befitting an adolescent bickering with his father. Maybe this person can learn to see his boss as less central in his life and find ways for parents and loved ones to nurture his self-esteem and positive feelings. His worklife should be just about business, and nothing personal.

Based on the above principles, as psychotherapists who also happen to be religious, we endeavor to never allow our personal and religious beliefs to intrude upon and interfere with the therapeutic process. On the other hand, it would be a mistake to discourage or avoid discussing religious issues to whatever extent they are of concern to the patient. Unfortunately though, this is what many therapists do out of a fear of being "nontherapeutic." However, this is a mistaken notion, as *anything* that is of concern to the patient should be discussed in therapy, and it is only the personal concerns and values of the therapist that should be kept in check. We have found it quite ironic that in certain clinical circles, though subject matter that most would find to be lurid and shocking is freely discussed and explored (as it rightfully should be in the name of science and understanding), the mere mention of religion is almost considered obscene. This is what we call the tyranny of the supposed liberal and openminded approach. Many followers of this approach are openminded to everything *except* religion. Why? Because religion, as they would accuse, is closeminded!

We are reminded of a true incident from a clinical graduate-school program that illustrates this point tragically. An Orthodox mother, and therapist-in-training, was censured by her professor for being irresponsible toward her clients by taking maternity leave during the training year. What was most odd and hypocritical is that in that very same class, there was a discussion defending the reproductive rights of mothers on welfare!

The essays in this book come out of our experience as religious Jews, parents, and psychotherapists. Any relation to actual people or families is truly coincidental. All of the vignettes are of a fictional and hypothetical nature. We believe that in order to sort out the many challenges that are faced by religious Jews today, it is necessary to have a better understanding of our religious values, our feelings, and the sociological dynamics that influence our culture. Our goals in these essays are to help address and clarify the many complex and interrelated issues that are a part of our lives today. When discussing religious issues, our intent is to educate people about ideas and concepts that may pertain to the problem, but not to provide halachic rulings. We hope that through this means, our readers will be better equipped to find the answers they seek.

In closing, we feel that the title of this book, *How to Have Fun without Getting into Trouble*, encapsulates a very serious conflict that most modern religious people have. Namely, how can they be emotionally free without compromising or violating their moral and religions convictions. Taken as a whole, we hope that the ideas in this book help guide the reader in answering this basic dilemma.

Readers who wish to contact us, may feel free to do so either through the publisher or via email: simcha_chaya@ excite.com

PART

I

❧

Relationships

1

꒰ᑲ

When You Can't Forgive

$\mathcal{M}$ost people abide by some basic religious ethic of forgiveness. According to the Jewish tradition, we should try to be forgiving of others in the hope that we also will be judged favorably for our sins. The Talmud (*Yoma* 87b) states: "One who overlooks his honor when offended will be forgiven for all his sins." In addition, according to the Jewish tradition, even though obtaining forgiveness is the sole responsibility of the offender, it is still considered cruel to withhold forgiveness from someone who is sincerely sorry. (See Maimonides, *Yad*, Laws of Repentance 2:10.)

However, forgiveness is a matter of the heart. What then, does a person who feels ethically and religiously bound to forgive do, when despite his best efforts, he cannot bring himself to forgive? Certainly, there are some offenses that are so horrible and hurtful that it may take years, if not a lifetime to erase. In such cases, some might not be troubled by the fact that they are unwilling to do so. Some may feel entitled to remain angry, and do not feel any obligation to be forgiving. On the other hand, others may feel guilty and dismayed that they are unable to let go and forgive, wishing somehow that they could forget the terrible offense, and yet are unable to do so. It is for the latter group that this is written.

SORTING IT OUT:

When it comes to major offenses, in order to be free to truly forgive, it is helpful to sort out the nature of the offense. The following questions should be answered:

1. Looking at the situation objectively, is the offense something that most people would be equally hurt by, or is it something that is subjective and specific to your circumstances?
2. Is there something concrete that can be done to rectify the hurt?
3. Does the person seem sincere in his apology?

The above factors are all related and critical to your being able to forgive. Most people need a sincere apology, which by definition includes both a feeling that the offending party understands the nature and extent of what has occurred, and that the person has taken steps to ensure that he won't hurt you again. Clearly, without some form of apology and effort to rectify matters, it is even harder to forgive. Though some religions may expect a person to forgive an offense even if no apology is offered, the Jewish tradition is refreshing in its realistic approach to the limits of emotional tolerance. In fact, when someone offends you, it is a moral obligation to inform him of your feelings. The great medieval Talmudist philosopher and physician, Maimonides, (*Yad*, Laws of Knowledge *Deos*, 6:6) states: "When one person wrongs another, the latter should not remain silent and despise him. This is the way of the wicked, as Samuel II (13:22) states: 'And Absalom did not speak to Amnon neither good nor bad, for Absalom hated Amnon.' Rather, one is commanded to make the matter known and ask him, 'Why did you do this to me?' 'Why did you wrong me regarding that matter?' "

In addition, be sure to articulate what *specifically* bothered you. Otherwise, if there is an aspect to your hurt that is not obvious, though the other person is apologizing, it will seem to you to be lacking in sincerity. This person will be unable to give you the feeling that he will be careful to prevent a reoccurrence, since he may not be aware of the full extent of the damage. Furthermore, if you want some kind of concrete action taken to help ameliorate your hurt feelings and he does not do it, it will be difficult to wholeheartedly forgive him.

For example, Shirley embarrassed Debbie publicly by making a joke about her clothes. Shirley realized that she hurt Debbie and she apologized, yet Debbie is still unable to forgive her. What Shirley does not know is that aside from the objective reality that she embarrassed Debbie, this embarrassment also had an especially hurtful effect due to particular circumstances from Debbie's past. Debbie used to be overweight as a child, and was taunted by her classmates. When Shirley made this flippant remark, it brought back Debbie's painful memories, and was subjectively far more embarrassing. Taking this into account, it is no wonder Shirley's apology does not feel "true" or satisfying to Debbie. Shirley is giving a "twenty-five-watt" apology for something that was experienced as a "one-hundred-megawatt" humiliation! In order for Debbie to really forgive Shirley, she must explain the extent of how she was hurt, and the circumstances that contributed to it. Indeed, the Talmud acknowledges that the same action can cause greater embarrassment to one person than another, and based on this, the victim may be entitled to greater or lesser financial compensation. (See *Bava Kamma* 83b. Note: This reference is for illustrative purposes only. Actually, the Tal-

CHAPTER

2

୬

How to Have a Fight with Your Spouse: Psychological and Religious Perspectives

*S*ome couples fight a little, some fight a lot. Perhaps there is a couple out there who never fights at all. But most people, once in a while, get into an argument or fight with their spouse. Hurtful things are said. Perhaps there is shouting; perhaps the children overhear and are frightened. Resentments build up and grudges may be held. Sometimes, resentment grows to the point where it cannot be repaired.

Can fighting solve anything? Can fights be good? If fighting solves problems, is there a better way to fight?

We believe that it is natural for two people who live together to have disagreements. Even major disagreements, with serious anger and resentment. The difference between a healthy, thriving relationship and a frozen, bitter relationship is how these frictions are dealt with. Anger can be a force for personal progress, growth, and change if channeled effectively. If your arguments follow the rules below, then you have a tool for improving your relationship instead of damaging it.

9

THE RULES:

Rule #1:

When you find yourself angry with your spouse, do not jump into action. If you are going to be successful, you must first better understand your state of mind by following the rules below.

Rule #2:

Now you must try to understand what exactly it is that you are angry about. This seems simple, but it is not. For example, you are about to drive somewhere and you find the tank of gas is near empty. You are annoyed and think, "Why does it always fall on me to fill the tank?" Or, you are upset because you feel that your spouse spent too much money on a gift for a relative. If, at this point, you go into a tirade, it may obscure the underlying problem. Namely, is it really just this chore, or are you feeling in general that too many chores are being burdened on you? Is the issue that there is not enough money, or do you feel bad that not enough of the family money is being spent on *you*? It is critical that you first honestly identify for yourself, as clearly as possible, what the issue *really* is. This way, the full force of your anger and upset can be brought to bear directly on the problem. Otherwise, you run the risk of being frustrated by an explanation that does not resolve the basic issue, that is, your spouse might give you a good explanation why the amount spent on the gift was appropriate.

Rule #3:

Never, ever, criticize or denigrate. If you are arguing with your spouse, you obviously are attempting to communicate with someone who you believe cares about your situation and has the ability to work to resolve it. When you criticize someone, you are not speaking to the part of him or her that can help you most. Therefore, only mention what is bothering you and how you feel about it. Do not mention how you feel toward the person who is bothering you.

Using the case examples above, you might say, "I hate being stuck with so many chores." Or, "It really bothers me to see so much money was spent on someone else when I feel that I need the money for my things." Instead of, "You are such an irresponsible person. . . ." That way, you have not said anything bad about the other person.

Rule #4:

Do not start arguing until you have determined that it is a good time. Most often, when we start fights it is when everyone is tense, privacy is scarce, and our stress level is high. You must note what you are mad about, and tell your spouse that something is bothering you and that you would like to find a time where it can be discussed in privacy and without other distractions.

In relationships, timing is everything, and this has long been recognized in the Jewish tradition.

One might compare this in concept to the rabbinic dictum in *The Chapters of our Fathers* (4:18) "Do not ask forgiveness from someone while he is still angry." The implication of this being, there are definitely better or worse times to work on solving disagreements.

Rule #5:

State what is upsetting you, then stop talking and really listen. It is crucial that after you make your point, you are ready to hear the response. Do not let your anger block receptivity to another person's point of view. If the response still does not satisfy you, first make it clear to your spouse that you listened to his or her point by repeating what was said; then state your objection (again following the rules). Using the case examples above, you might say, "I agree with you that you have a lot of burdens at work, but somehow I still feel that I need more help with the chores." Or, "I hear what you are saying, that in fact, you did buy me a big birthday gift last year. But I am referring to the fact that on a daily basis there is not enough money to buy smaller things."*Always remember to preface your response with a summation of your spouse's.*

Rule #6:

Know when to quit. Step number five can be repeated as long as both parties continue to hear each others' points and respond flexibly and thoughtfully. If, for whatever reason, this process shuts down and you do not feel your spouse is listening or responding fairly, call a time-out. File the problem away and bring it up at a later time. DO NOT start fighting about how your spouse isn't listening! Just forget the issue for the time being. Don't worry, because in relationships most problems are of a thematic and cyclical nature. This issue will come up again soon, and you will have your chance to discuss it again.

Rule #7:

It is OK to be mad. When you are saying what is bothering you, if you follow the rules, the anger will not be destructive. To the contrary, if you are really angry, it will impress upon your spouse how truly upset you are, and it will focus your feelings. But please be careful, because if you do not follow the above rules, the intensity of the anger can be misdirected and cause serious damage.

SAMPLE DIALOGUES:

Wrong way:

"You are so sloppy! I can't take it when you leave the toothpaste uncovered. I'm tired of this! Do you hear me? Are you even listening . . .?"

Right way, using the rules:

"I am really upset about something, but I want to find a time to talk when we are both calm and able to work it through." [Once the time is found:] "When the toothpaste is left uncovered it makes me so angry. I am very, very angry, because I feel that I have too much work to do around this house. [Do not state that others in the house are lazy. There is no need to criticize others; they can draw their own conclusions about their laziness. It will needlessly distract and cause arguments.] (You should now be quiet after stating clearly what is bothering you, and wait for a response, instead of continuing a tirade.)

As a final point, keep in mind that we are not attempting to definitively guide anyone morally. We are just describing what seems to be effective from a human relations perspective. A person may object to the whole idea of arguing, anger, and fighting based on their particular values and understanding of their religious dictates. We encourage you to explore this further with your rabbi, and welcome additional comments in support, modification, or dissent of the ideas mentioned above.

However, [it is also worthwhile to note] that our approach would seem to be supported by some Jewish traditional sources. For example, as we quoted in Chapter One, Maimonides, (*Yad, Deos,* 6:6) states: "When one person wrongs another, the latter should not remain silent and despise him. This is the way of the wicked, as Samuel II (13:22) states: 'And Absalom did not speak to Amnon neither good nor bad, for Absalom hated Amnon.' Rather, one is commanded to make the matter known and ask him, 'Why did you do this to me?' 'Why did you wrong me regarding that matter?'"

Of course, some might feel that life would be great if no one ever disagreed or got angry. But, if you find yourself angry and upset with your spouse, by following these rules you can hopefully come to feel closer, and bring new levels of understanding to your relationship.

3

ॐ

Helping Someone Who is Self-Destructive

*I*t is hard to watch someone destroy himself. Unfortunately, we sometimes come across friends, relatives, or acquaintances that seem to be making all the wrong choices in life. The nature of self-destructiveness can be subtle, and not always obvious, especially to those who are most involved. Some examples include:

1. Someone who persistently neglects his diet and exercise, despite being in a coronary-risk category.
2. Someone who is unable to maintain a job due to "attitude problems."
3. Someone who seems unable to plan his career, and avoids making choices, even when offered help.
4. Someone who drives recklessly, or engages in similar risk-taking behavior.
5. Someone who mismanages his finances to a serious degree.

(Please note, in this chapter we are discussing how to deal with the more subtle forms of self-destructive behavior. If you know of someone who is overtly self-destructive, for example, suicidal, or engaging in alcohol or substance abuse, you should seek professional guidance immediately.)

To some extent, everyone engages in self-destructive behavior every now and then. However, a person with a self-destructive personality engages in a pervasive pattern of self-destructiveness. Often, the person himself is oblivious and will deny this behavior. He may say, "Nonsense. It's all under control." How do you diagnose a self-destructive personality? Ironically, the main symptom of his behavior is felt by the people who are close to him. *They* are the ones who are uneasy and nervous. If you find yourself persistently more worried, involved, and engaged in problem solving than the person you are trying to help, chances are, this person is being self-destructive.

Remember this fact: The major obstacle to helping someone who is self-destructive is that very person! Whether the reasons are apparent or not, such a person is unconsciously trying to harm or even destroy himself. Since the person is both trying to destroy himself, and at the same time unaware of this, it will obviously be difficult to get that person to stop.

THE ORIGIN OF SELF-DESTRUCTIVE BEHAVIOR:

Self-destructiveness may stem from unconscious sources, for example, guilt or anger. In general, feelings become submerged, or unconscious, as a defense mechanism because they may be too difficult to face outright. The guilt may be too difficult to bear without being crushed, so instead a person may submerge it and then punish himself over time, as a way of making amends. Or, regarding anger, many people find anger to be too dangerous to be felt outright, particularly in regard to anger felt toward a person they live with, or who is emotionally close to them. Once again, as an unconscious defense, a person may submerge the feeling below his awareness. Nevertheless, he may act out on this feeling by being self-destructive "Kamikaze style," in order to hurt a loved one by hurting himself. (In WWII, Kamikaze was the Japanese term for a soldier who would fly an airplane loaded with explosives into the enemy ships, killing himself, but causing significant damage to the enemy.) This kind of submerging of feelings happens most often in relationships where there are long-standing and unresolved problems. The person feels that his situation is hopeless and his anger is futile or that he has no constructive way to express his anger, just as a suicide bomber will kill himself in opposition to an impossibly stronger enemy.

WHAT YOU CAN DO:

How can you help someone who, whether he is aware of it or not, is in fact, planning his demise? The rabbis of the Talmud astutely observed, "It is forbidden to have mercy on a fool" (see Sanhedrin 92a).

If you suspect this person is acting out anger felt toward you, you can try to address it by improving your relationship. In many instances, it is difficult to see this kind of problem objectively, so you might be better off seeing a marital or family therapist. If all parties are emotionally mature and stable, it should only require a few sessions to improve communication significantly. Over time, this improvement of communication will allow a more appropriate and healthy outlet for the expression of resentment.

However, if you believe the problems have nothing to do with you and your relationship with this person, then you must take a different tactic:

The first step is to take a deep breath and slow down. As we mentioned earlier, it is the friends and loved ones that feel the most despair and distress, not the self-destructive person himself! Over time, this takes a heavy toll. Therefore, you must come to grips with the objective reality. Since you cannot effectively stop anyone from doing what he really wants to do, you must let go of your guilt and give up control. Obviously, you want to help save this person, but you cannot take upon yourself the impossible burden of trying to keep afloat someone who wants to drown!

On the other hand, since this person's behavior may be truly unconscious, you can't really blame him either. The goal is to help make him more aware of his unconscious destructive behavior, so he can be free to evaluate it and make better choices. The trick is to do it in a way that minimizes defensiveness and maximizes self-awareness.

FOLLOW THIS CARDINAL RULE:

Never let your level of interest or energy exceed the energy of the person you are helping. If you see that it is, do not get angry or criticize him. Instead, ask, in a genuine and curious tone, why this appears to be so. Then, be open to his response. Instead of endless nagging, both you and he may learn something new. In any case, at least you won't be wasting your time on a futile effort to artificially "prop up" someone who is not yet ready to change.

CASE SCENARIOS:

Case Scenario #1:

Joseph is having difficulty getting a job. His friend, Steven, offers to put aside time to help him with his résumé. When Steven comes over to help, Joseph is not prepared and seems to be distracted and uninvolved. Steven might ask, "This does not seem very important to you. I am curious why this is so, since it is a generally accepted idea that a good résumé is helpful in getting a job." This blunt, but not unnecessarily rude question may arouse Joseph to become more aware of his true feelings. He may say, "Because nothing ever works." This is important information. Steven can respond, "You sound depressed. No wonder why we aren't getting anywhere."

At this point, Steven should not proceed any further with work on the résumé until some progress is made on the depression. Steven has done all he can do; it is now up to Joseph to take the next steps. These steps may involve giving himself an internal "peptalk," or he may consider getting treatment, or another plan of action. The point is, Joseph should be involved in finding a solution and Steven ready to assist, instead of Steven pushing and prodding Joseph to help himself.

If Joseph continues to do nothing productive, but keeps asking Steven for "help," Steven should ask Joseph what kind of help he wants. If it makes sense, Steven should do it. If it is vague or without direction, Steven should encourage Joseph to clarify and be specific.

For example, Joseph might say, "I don't really know what kind of job I should do. Help me decide." Instead of jumping in and offering all kinds of suggestions, Steven should ask, "What did you have in mind when you asked me to help you decide?" After all, how is Steven supposed to know what kind of job Joseph would want? After this kind of discussion, it may emerge that there actually is some way that Steven could help Joseph decide. Maybe Joseph is curious about how Steven decided on his own career. However, this kind of productive level of interest will be more likely to emerge only if Steven is restrained in his efforts to "help," and waits for Joseph to continue to struggle to explain exactly what kind of help he wants.

Case Scenario #2:

Rebecca hates watching her husband overeat. The doctor already warned him that his cholesterol is too high. Rebecca tries planning diets, special menus, and other incentives for her husband. Still, no matter what she does, he'll order in Chinese food at work, or overeat at social events.

Rebecca should try to discuss the facts neutrally. She might say at a calm moment, "Mark, I notice that you do not seem so interested in keeping your diet. Based on what Dr. X says, it seems you are endangering your health. I don't think I can force you to eat right; however, we must consider the sober reality of the situation. Your life is in danger. Do we have enough life insurance? Seriously, I mean, if you are going to kill yourself slowly, I cannot stop you, but I want to be sure that the children will be properly provided for. Also, I think we should discuss cemetery plots and funeral arrangements. You know how much of a burden those things can be when left for the last minute. . . ."

Strange as this may seem, if Rebecca can really pull this off without sounding hostile, she has a chance of helping Mark become aware of his unconscious desire to slowly kill himself. Furthermore, why should Rebecca spend her energy chasing after Mark to work on his diet if he doesn't care? She might as well nag him about something more practical that he is willing to take care of, such as, his life insurance and funeral arrangements! Be careful though, this tactic can only work if Rebecca is genuine and not sarcastic. Sarcasm will only arouse defensiveness and hostility.

CONCLUDING THOUGHTS:

In summary, in order to help someone who is unconsciously resisting help, you must be careful not to get overinvolved. You must be able to give helpful feedback, and be ready to pull back when the person does not appear to be interested. This does not mean you shouldn't be compassionate, just be sure that your compassion and energy are not misdirected or wasted. Once again, the rabbis say it best: "If you are inappropriately merciful when you should be harsh, one day you will end up being harsh when you should be merciful." (*Koheles Rabbah* Commentary on Ecclesiastes, 7:16.) The meaning of this is, if a person expends his energies and compassion in an inappropriate manner, the resulting frustration and dissatisfaction will drive him to take it out on an innocent party.

4

✌

Living with a "Control Freak" and How Not to Be a Controlling Person

*W*hat is a "control freak?" Of course, the term is not a technical one. Nevertheless, it has a definite meaning and is referring to a particular kind of personality, what some would call a controlling person. The clinical term for this condition is "Obsessive Compulsive Personality Disorder."

(This should not be confused with the much more serious Obsessive Compulsive Disorder, otherwise known as OCD. People who suffer from OCD are compulsively locked into repetitive rituals or behaviors to ward off upsetting thoughts, such as constant hand-washing out of an imagined obsessional fear of germs. This is a more severe condition, and its etiology is not necessarily related to Obsessive Compulsive Personality Disorder.)

Do You:

1. Need to have everything planned out perfectly before you go on a trip?

2. Worry about running out of things and need to have emergency supplies?
3. Get anxious and irritable when you enter into situations that you cannot completely control?
4. Worry about money?
5. Get impatient with people who are not "perfect?"
6. Have difficulty delegating tasks and trusting others to "do it the right way?"
7. Feel extremely uncomfortable taking risks?
8. Do people around you find you to be stubborn, exacting, and perfectionistic, when to you it seems that you are just being responsible and careful?

If you have answered "yes" to four or more of these questions, you may be suffering from Obsessive Compulsive Personality Disorder. As with most personality disorders, the person who has the disorder suffers the least. And actually, it is the people who live with the person that suffer the most. So, don't be surprised if you are not troubled much by these symptoms. After all, *It's not your fault that no one else knows how to do it as well as you do.* (Is that line of thought familiar to you?)

What usually drives people with Obsessive Compulsive Personality Disorder to seek treatment is a culmination of many interpersonal and relationship failures whereby the person begins to get an inkling that something might be amiss. To illustrate, this person might be failing in his relationship with his spouse and/or children, or be "inexplicably" overlooked for a promotion at work despite doing a "perfect job." What he does not realize is that his perfectionism creates a barrier between him and other people. It makes them uncomfortable, resentful, and jealous. At first, he will assume it's "everyone else's problem," but over time, even a "control freak" may concede that he might be contributing to the problem. (Please note: We use the masculine pronoun out of convenience. This disorder is also present in the female population.)

THE ORIGINS OF PERFECTIONISM:

As we will mention many times in this book, the drive to achieve competence and control is a basic human trait. What goes wrong in a person who is overly perfectionistic, is that he has used his natural talents and ability to be nearly perfect, as a way of avoiding the anxiety and stress of inevitable failures. This becomes a self-reinforcing behavior pattern, where more and more of life's anxieties are deflected by an endless quest to control them.

People who have Obsessive Compulsive personalities may manifest their need to control in their choice of profession. Such persons may be unconsciously drawn to particular professions because they allow an illusion of control, by being authorities over a particular sphere of the human condition. To illustrate, a person may choose to become a doctor because of an unconscious fear of illness and a need to have mastery over disease. (Of course, we do not intend to cast a disparaging light on any one particular choice of profession, as this controlling behavior can be acted out in almost any profession.)

WHAT YOU CAN DO:

As a control freak, the last thing you will want to do is to turn your fate over to someone else and seek professional help. You probably think that you are smart enough to solve the problem on your own. Well, you *are* smart, and no one is questioning that. After all, you have been able to be nearly perfect and in control for a long time. Unfortunately, a person cannot easily see his own flaws. Additionally, part of your recovery is acknowledging that you cannot control everything yourself. Therefore, we strongly advise you to seek treatment and to be patient. If you really are interested in improving the quality of your life, you will need to work with the therapist in an open, cooperative, and collaborative manner. Do not jump to conclusions and assume you know everything. If you have questions and complaints about your treatment, explore them with your therapist instead of assuming he is wrong and seeking out a new and more "perfect" therapist.

Recognizing that a controlling person is almost addicted to his behavior, we know you can't go "cold turkey." So, we will give you some treatment pointers for you to consider while you are trying to find the "perfect" and "best" therapist. (By the way, though of course you should find the most competent therapist that you can, no therapist will understand you all the time. In fact, a key component of some forms of treatment involve working out these misunderstandings ["empathic breaks"] between the therapist and the patient, because they are often emblematic and representative of deeper hurts from early childhood.)

The correct developmental path is to learn to tolerate ambiguity, risk, and failure. After all, we cannot truly and absolutely control our fates. We can suffer mishaps and die at any moment. Can you imagine an infant ever learning how to walk if he became of afraid of what will happen if he falls? You need to work on strengthening your ability to tolerate mistakes in yourself and others. Next time you make a mistake, instead of blaming yourself or someone else, accept it and laugh!

STRATEGIES ON HOW TO LIVE WITH A CONTROLLING PERSON:

Earlier we noted that those who live with and are emotionally close to a controlling person are the ones who suffer the most. In fact, most controlling people assume that "everyone else has the problem." Of course, technically, they are correct. After all, they are "perfect." Is it their fault that we cannot do it the "right way?" Of course, this makes it extremely challenging for the regular mortals who must live with Mr. or Mrs. Perfect.

At times, you will be made to feel foolish, immature, irresponsible, wasteful, impulsive, and dumb. If you react with anger or spite, that only gives this person more evidence to use against you. If you try to argue for doing it your way, you cannot win, since "logic" is on the side of perfection. How can you successfully argue to spend more money, or to engage in *less* planning, without sounding irresponsible and careless? On paper, the controlling person will always win. It is difficult to capture the intangible value of flexibility, spontaneity, and adventure in a strictly rational analysis.

To survive this kind of relationship, you must first enter into the "control freak's" world and stake out some territory of your own.

UNDERSTANDING THE
CONTROLLING PERSONALITY:

A person who suffers from Obsessive Compulsive Personality Disorder experiences extreme anxiety when he is in situations that he cannot control. By the way, this person may be completely unaware that he fears anxiety. In fact, he may appear to be the epitome of calm. Developmentally, this person was not able to learn to fully tolerate uncertainty and ambiguity; he thus uses the illusion of control and perfection to calm and soothe his anxiety. You cannot change this, you can only accept this as a fact of living with this person. (*He* could change it, by entering into treatment. But he probably won't, because he is "perfect already." Do not get your hopes up on convincing this person, as it takes a tremendous amount of sober and honest self-assessment for such a person to be willing to enter therapy.)

Recognizing these basic personality issues, you need to give this person as much control as possible, without having it completely obliterate your own personal freedom of choice. You will need to make it clear that you understand how critical and important it is that he be in control over this area, and still ask him if there is a way he can see allowing you to do it "your way," even if it might lead to "disaster." You will need to pick and choose your battles, and patiently, over time, "chisel out" areas where you can convince him to let go of his control.

SAMPLE DIALOGUE:

Nathan feels that every particular detail of the trip must be planned. This includes the financial aspects and the itinerary. After all, without proper precautions and planning, things could "get out of control." Nathan wants everything to be "perfect" for his long-awaited vacation.

Esther goes on vacation to have fun. She thinks Nathan's idea of a vacation is just more work. What's the point in going away if you have to plan everything?

Esther must realize that she cannot redo Nathan's personality overnight. But she can work with his need to control by bringing up many of her concerns in advance and allowing Nathan to at least maintain some control by *planning for the unplanned*. She might say, "Look, Nathan. I know you feel we must plan every detail of this trip. However, I like to do things spontaneously, and that is *my* idea of a "perfect" vacation. I like the adventure of getting a little lost and discovering something new. Is it OK if we plan one day to be a "free day?" This way, we can put aside some extra money and time to allow me to wander around and do whatever comes to mind."

This strategy is likely to work because it gives Nathan the maximum amount of control while still allowing Esther some freedom from his oppressive vacation schedule.

CONCLUDING THOUGHTS:

Over time, if you keep negotiating in this manner, you can accomplish two things:

1. Carve out some space for yourself, where you are not subject to your partner's exacting standards.
2. Gradually teach your partner greater tolerance for the imperfect and the unplanned.

5

ᘓᘏ

Doubts in
Dating and Marriage

*I*f you are dating someone seriously and are unable to decide if he or she is the right one to marry, you may have already asked friends, family, or your rabbi for advice. However, if after thinking about it and talking it over and listening to common-sense suggestions, you still feel stuck and unsure of what to decide, you may need to look at some deeper psychological issues.

Keep in mind, each religious community and strata of observance may have a different definition for what is "taking too long to decide." A less traditional and more secular person may consider dating the same person for several years as normal, and for that person it is (at least, from a mental-health perspective). On the other end of the spectrum, someone from an extremely "yeshivish" or "Chassidish" family, might feel that it is not normal to be unable to decide after only four dates! Both examples are valid, and the issues remain the same. This is because a person's goal should be to function in an emotionally healthy manner within one's familial and cultural context. Therefore, the psychologies behind these difficulties are still essentially identical.

DOUBTS:

The first area to consider is the nature of the doubts that you are experiencing. Do these doubts seem to have an objective rational basis, or are they more subjective and idiosyncratic? Understanding the nature of the doubt is an important clue to unraveling this knotty decision.

Examples of a Rational Objective Doubt:

1. I get along well with him, but I worry about our future together because he does not have a clear career goal.
2. I enjoy spending time with her, but she has a mild medical condition that could become worse.
3. He/she is fifteen years older/younger than I.

If your doubts fit into the above category, we have good news and bad news. The good news is, you probably do not have any deep psychological issues with marriage and commitment. The bad news is, you have what's known as an existential dilemma. Simply put, there is no clear answer and you must struggle to decide what is best. Ultimately, you will be the one to bear the consequences with whatever choice you make. There may be no "right" decision, as there are potential gains and losses in each case. It is understandable that in such a case you would have difficulty deciding what to do. However, at some point, all adults must make difficult decisions.

Nevertheless, be advised, if you still find yourself unable to come to a decision for a protracted period of time, you may have a secondary emotional complication that is blocking or weakening your confidence and resolve. For example, you may actually know in your heart what you want to do, but are afraid of what people will think, and especially afraid of having to hear "I told you so" if it turns out you are wrong. Consider the example of choosing to marry someone who is much older or younger. It might indeed be foolish to turn down marrying your "soulmate" solely due to age difference, but you must still be prepared to tolerate others' disapproval as you venture beyond the community norms. It takes a person who has self-confidence to do what he thinks is best, even if it is not the popular route. Of course, this is merely an example of what may be a sound decision and not a confirmation that in all cases this kind of marriage is a wise choice. After all, community norms are in place for a reason. These norms represent the collective wisdom of the community, based on its acquired experiences. So don't try something different unless you are positive about the overriding nature of your individual circumstances.

In a case where you do not feel confident enough to make your decision, discussing the matter with an objective and neutral third party, such as a therapist, can be helpful. In addition, seeing a therapist may be beneficial because this inability to decide may be a symptom of a general weakness in your self-confidence. Getting treatment to improve your confidence can only enhance your relationship with whomever you ultimately choose to marry.

Examples of Subjective and Idiosyncratic Doubt:

1. We get along well, and she is good-looking, but I do not find myself attracted to her.
2. Everyone says he is perfect for me, and we have a lot in common, but there are no "fireworks."
3. We get along great, but we are from very different backgrounds.

If your doubts fit the above category, you may be dealing with an internal psychological issue. This is because when someone is conflicted about a matter of preference and unable to resolve it after an appropriate amount of careful consideration, there is often an underlying contributing unconscious dynamic. As much as it may seem to you to be about this issue, it may in fact be an expression of other unconscious conflicts. For example:

1. You may have a need to be rebellious. This means you may either really want to marry this person, but it irritates you that he/she is too "regular." Or, you may be choosing someone specifically because he/she is a little bit "different," in order to rebel and challenge those around you. Since your main attraction to this person is out of a need that is secondary to actual personal preference, you might sense this deep down, and have second thoughts about your choice.

2. Alternatively, you may have an overly compliant personality, which can complicate your choice of a spouse. You may feel conflicted about whether you are choosing this person out of a need to make your family happy, or out of genuine attraction and compatibility.

3. Lastly, you might be unconsciously afraid of commitment and responsibility, and be hiding behind a "smoke screen" of some other objection. It may be easier to say you don't like a certain feature about your potential mate, than face the difficulty of making a life-altering decision. By the way, this is not to say that you should ignore this fear of commitment and responsibility and get married anyway. Rather, you should be honest about it and try to address it in a meaningful and productive manner. Unconscious conflicts vary from person to person, based on emotional development, character structure, and internal defenses. We cannot adequately address this problem, save to illustrate the concept in broad terms. If you find yourself stuck on this kind of issue, even one or two sessions with a therapist can be very helpful.

PARENTAL APPROVAL/DISAPPROVAL:

This may sound old-fashioned, but parental approval is critical for a successful marriage. Though one certainly has the right to choose to marry anyone whom he sees fit, on a practical level, disapproving parents of either spouse can easily destroy a relationship. Therefore, should you be contemplating marrying someone of whom either set of parents disapprove, proceed with caution.

In a case where one or both sets of parents disapprove of the match, the optimal solution would be to attempt to patiently hear and address the nature of the objections. Even if it will take an extra period of time to satisfy the objecting party's concerns, it is a worthwhile investment. If there are concerns about the nature of someone's religiosity, character, ability to earn enough money to help support a family, family background, and so forth, do not put pressure on the situation or turn it into a power struggle. Obviously, as an adult, you have the right to marry whomever you choose. Nevertheless, you should allow your parents/future in-laws the time it takes to get to know you/your potential mate better, so they can feel more comfortable with the decision. Keep in mind that this process may take time, and may not work at all. If you resent being controlled and being pressured to wait, that is certainly understandable. However, it is a true kindness for your potential mate, parents, future in-laws, as well as yourself, to try in every way possible to work out the issue. Try to involve a neutral third party to act as a mediator, such as a rabbi whom everyone respects.

If ultimately nothing works, and you feel that you must go ahead anyway, despite how either set of parents feels, be advised that it will be a much greater challenge to have a successful marriage under those circumstances. You and your potential mate might feel right now that nothing can ever come between you; however, we have seen how, years later, serious complications arise in marriages made under the shadow of parental disapproval. This is not to say that such a marriage is guaranteed to fail, just that one must be fully apprised of the risk to benefit ratio when making such decisions.

DANGER SIGNS:

There are universal danger signs that one should not ignore, and which weigh heavily on the side of terminating a relationship should they be present—even if you are already engaged. After all, breaking an engagement is still easier and less painful than a divorce:

1. He or she has a violent temper. Remember, the key to any successful relationship is the ability to talk through and work things out even when under pressure.
2. He or she is physically or verbally abusive.
3. A major area of trust has been violated, for example, if he/she spent a large sum of money that you both had agreed on saving, or she/he humiliated you by speaking badly about you in front of others. (What is considered "a breach of trust" can be highly subjective, so don't jump to conclusions without carefully listening to the other side.)
4. If you find yourselves going through "roller-coaster" emotional states, for example, if you find that as a couple you alternate between being intensely in love and fighting intensely. (This last example is a sign of underlying emotional issues that should be addressed in therapy. Untreated, it will probably repeat itself should you later find a different mate.)

If staying together is of paramount importance, despite the danger signs, you should definitely seek competent premarital counseling to work out these issues before you get married.

A WORD OF CAUTION TO MARRIED COUPLES:

The above-mentioned indicators are designed to help a person decide on whom to choose or not choose as a mate. However, if you fear that you have already married someone who is not compatible with you, it certainly is worth spending some time trying to resolve the problems with a competent therapist first, before seeking to end the relationship.

6

The Psychology of In-law Conflicts

$\mathcal{H}$aving a good relationship with your in-laws is a cornerstone for a healthy marriage. Difficult as this may be to achieve for some, we believe that there are few exceptions to this rule. This is true even in situations where your spouse does not get along well with his or her parents, as we will discuss later on.

Why is this so important? Because every child has a strong emotional bond with his or her parents, no matter how it may seem on the surface. Even a person who claims that he hates his parents or has no feelings for them, is only expressing one emotion among many that he feels toward his parents. In almost all cases, no matter what has transpired, there will always remain a need to have a connection with one's parents. A marriage can either be strengthened by taking advantage of this bond, or weakened by fighting against it. No one should have to choose between loving their parents or loving their spouse. When people are forced to choose, the end result is never comfortable or satisfying.

In this article we will discuss the origins of some typical in-law problems, and what can be done about them.

WHOSE VALUES WILL ENDURE?

To better understand in-law problems, it is important to realize what basic issue is behind most areas of interfamilial conflict. In a certain sense, each family can be viewed as a nation unto itself, with its own particular culture and customs. When a child gets married, two "nations" must join together and form an alliance. In this process, there is an instinctive struggle for the continuity of the values and mores of each nation. It is an emotionally stressful experience for a parent to let go of the child he or she has raised, and hand him or her over to a "foreigner." Of course, most families are flexible enough to make the emotional transition that is necessary to partially let go of one of their own "citizens," and to allow new "citizens" to "immigrate" into the system. In addition, there is a natural give-and-take as the two "nations" blend together. Common ground is found, and if accommodations are necessary, certain rules, values, and customs are modified and adjusted. However, many in-law problems can be seen to contain shades or aspects of the following basic unvoiced questions: "Whose values will endure? Which family will have itself replicated in the future generation?"

For example, conflicts about where you will live, what school your children will go to, how your children should behave, and what careers you will choose, are all really about who gets to control and shape the future generation. Parents invest an incalculable amount of energy in the nurturing and education of their children, and it is only natural that they develop an almost territorial stance regarding their offspring. When you view things from this perspective, many seemingly petty arguments are understandable. If you and your spouse find yourselves arguing about matters such as these, you have unwittingly become pawns in this tribal war over the future generation. Each of you is now charged with the duty of continuing your family's heritage. It is difficult to have a rational discussion when you feel like a traitor to your family of origin. If you want to survive a conflict such as this, you will need to learn to be objective about the situation.

As is the case with most conflicts, a person's ability to think rationally is greatly compromised by tension and stress. If you can find a way to reduce the pressure of the conflicting loyalties that your spouse may be feeling, he or she may become more emotionally free and available to see things from your perspective. This can be understood by way of a metaphor. It is much harder to untangle a rope when people are pulling hard on both ends. However, if the rope is loosened, it is easier to untangle. So too, with human conflicts. If there is an emotional "tug of war," it is very hard for the parties involved to untangle the knots. Therefore, if you are stubborn and insist on pulling on your spouse's loyalty from one end, and his or her parents are pulling on the other end, it is very hard to unravel the mess and see matters clearly and objectively. You can't count on the other party to be reasonable and loosen the rope, so you must let some of the pressure off your spouse. Accomplishing this, requires practice, patience, and proper technique.

So what can you do? The first thing you must do is to enlist your spouse's cooperation:

1. Acknowledge that your spouse naturally feels a need to please and comply with his or her parent's wishes.
2. Ask your spouse whether he or she is open to hearing why you disagree with them and wish to do things differently. You should inform your spouse that your goal is just to discuss what the two of you think would be the best approach, assuming you both felt free to make any decision, independent of parental influences and wishes. You should be sure to make it perfectly clear that you

have no intention of forcing your spouse to disrespect or disobey his or her parents.

This approach works because, by indicating your understanding and support for your spouse's need to remain allied with his or her parents, you will ease your spouse's tension and struggle over loyalty. Returning to the "rope metaphor," it is much harder to untangle a rope when people are pulling hard on both ends. However, once the rope is loosened, it is easier to untangle. So too, with human conflicts. If there is an emotional "tug of war," it is very hard for the parties involved to untangle the knots. If you are pulling on your spouse's loyalty from one end, and his or her parents are pulling on the other end, it is very hard to unravel the mess and see matters clearly and objectively.

You might find at this point, if you have achieved steps one and two, that there is a possibility for compromise. Once your spouse has your emotional support and backing, he or she may even come to agree with your view and wish to differ from his or her parents' view. You can then strategize how to do it in the least offensive manner. In most cases, if both spouses are in agreement, and the matter is discussed respectfully but with firm resolve, in-laws will back off and let their children run their own lives. Be advised however, that there are exceptions, and in cases where in-laws seem to be unable to tolerate disagreement or separation from their children, family counseling may be necessary.

IF YOU ARE THE SPOUSE WHO FEELS CONFLICTED ABOUT FAMILY LOYALTY:

Similar to the rope metaphor explained above, as long as there is tension on both sides, no one can undo the knots. As long as your spouse is pulling hard for your loyalty, there will be no hope in enlisting his or her cooperation. Though we understand that you are in a difficult position, and may even feel that your spouse is utterly wrong and your parents are completely right, you will have to modify your approach. Unless you are married to a saint, no spouse can indefinitely endure the perception that he or she is second rate to his or her in-laws. Of course, you may feel that your spouse's position is unreasonable and petty, and why can't he or she just "go along" with what your parents want, at least for your sake? The answer is, he or she probably can. The problem is, this petty thing has become a symbolic struggle for your love and loyalty. Unless you can reassure your spouse of your loyalty, the argument and struggle will continue. However, you can work together to sort out diplomatic solutions most of the time, as long as you are cooperating as a team. The only way to do this though, is to elicit your spouse's cooperation. This will be much more likely to happen if you can reassure your spouse of your loyalty toward him or her. To do this, you must communicate to your spouse, in no uncertain terms, that you will always side with him or her in front of your parents. This may be very hard for you to agree to do. Nevertheless, in the long run, you will cause less hurt to everyone involved. You can try to explain in advance your new approach to your parents. This way, you may be able to elicit some understanding and patience. You also should inform your spouse that, although when "push comes to shove" you will take his or her side, it will be extremely painful to you and you would like to avoid having to do this by trying to come up with some reasonable compromises.

If you have been paying close attention to this article, you may have noticed that the suggestions we give to each kind of spouse are not interdependent. In fact, each strategy assumes that the other is either unwilling or incapable of changing. As is often the case in conflicts, there may initially be only one party who is bighearted enough to make the first move. These interventions are designed to help facilitate that first step, with the hope that once the tension and conflict are reduced, both parties will be able to be more objective and supportive.

WHEN YOUR SPOUSE DOES NOT GET ALONG WITH HIS OR HER PARENTS:

When your spouse does not get along with his or her parents, you may have an urge to join the fight. Particularly if they say things that hurt your spouse, you will have your own pride at stake and feel compelled to strike back. Though your spouse may even express a desire for you to join him or her in this conflict, or perhaps to defend him or her, or to criticize his or her parents, that would be a dangerous thing to do. This can be compared to the cultural reality that members of a minority group can share racial jokes and epithets that humorously satirize or stereotype them. On the other hand, should someone outside of the group use those same jokes and epithets, disastrous results will ensue. A similar dynamic can occur within a family. Your in-laws might find your spouse's criticisms and lack of respect to be much more tolerable than anything you might say. This is because, similar to the example above of racial jokes, you are the "outsider" and perceived in a more hostile and threatening light—even if that is not your intention.

The approach you must take is as follows:

1. Express your support and sympathy for your spouse's experience. Try to help ease the hurt of whatever insult was endured.
2. Later, when your spouse has calmed down, try to encourage your spouse to improve his or her relationship with his parents. (See *Pirkei Avos* 4:18, "Do not attempt to calm your friend at the moment of his anger.") If the relationship is highly conflictual, you should encourage him or her to seek counseling.

This strategy will help you to avoid being blamed as an instigator and outsider who brought problems into the family. In addition, should things improve, you will have had a hand in this and be even more endeared to all parties.

Sample Scenario:

Sarah finds that whenever Yossi's mother needs help with something, he drops everything and goes running. This really angers her, because Yossi is not very helpful to her with her needs. In the past, when Sarah would complain, Yossi would get mad and they would just end up fighting.

Yossi is stuck in a loyalty bind between his duties as a son and as a husband. He may find it difficult or impossible to say "no" to his mother, and find it painful to disappoint his wife. Using the rope metaphor once again, when a rope is pulled taut from both directions it is impossible to untangle the knots! Though Sarah may be completely justified in her complaints, Sarah is pulling on Yossi's loyalty in the other direction. The result is excruciating tension for Yossi. As with many people who experience tension, his reaction is anger and irrational behavior.

In order for Sarah to get relief from this problem, she needs to be willing to loosen the rope and "cut Yossi some slack." This does not mean letting him off the hook entirely. Sarah has the right to expect her husband's assistance and cooperation, and certainly should confront Yossi about this problem. However, she cannot expect him to respond when he is being pulled so strongly in both directions. The key is the technique:

1. First Sarah should join Yossi in helping his mother. Whatever the past history is, and whatever resentment Sarah may feel, she will change her relationship dynamics dramatically by doing this. Sarah should tell Yossi, "I know you feel that your mother needs a lot of help. I care about

what you care about. In fact, I want to join you in helping your mother." Sarah should accompany and assist
Yossi in whatever chore or task he is engaged in.

2. Having accomplished this, meaning, having given Yossi
    the breathing room of not being stuck in a loyalty bind,
    Sarah may find Yossi to be newly receptive to her con-
    cerns. Sarah can then broach the idea with Yossi that,
    though she is completely in favor of helping out Mom,
    there are many things around the house that are being
    neglected. She should ask Yossi to work with her to-
    gether on planning how both needs can be met. Para-
    doxically, the more Sarah indicates she is in favor of
    helping out Yossi's mother, the more likely he will be
    receptive to helping out Sarah. Even if Sarah does not
    really feel this way, it would help if she ended off the
    conversation with a statement such as, "Yossi, though I
    believe we must take care of our own household, I also
    feel that taking care of your mother should be an equal
    priority, so let's work on this together."

An Added Bonus:
Oddly, when loyalty conflicts and tensions are reduced, sometimes people will change their minds completely. In the scenario
above, Sarah may be surprised to find that as she becomes a
strong proponent of helping out Yossi's mother, Yossi may on
his own decide that he is doing too much for his mother, and
too little for his wife. This is because once freed from the loyalty bind, a person is able to see a situation more objectively.

If you take steps to actively loosen and relieve the loyalty
conflicts that are inherent in most in-law difficulties, you will
find that the situation can be improved dramatically. Remember, in order to succeed, someone has to be willing to "let go
of the rope" first. Though it may feel unfair and be difficult to
do, the rewards will outweigh the cost.

7

ॐ

Being Smart
Isn't Everything

No one can argue that intelligence is not an important asset. However, as psychotherapists, we have found it to be highly overrated when it comes to success in certain areas of life. This is particularly true when it comes to relationships. Often, individuals who are highly capable and successful in their academic and professional pursuits remain utterly lost and clueless when it comes to interpersonal relationships.

"BUT IT DOESN'T MAKE SENSE!"

Many couples and families have conflicts over a particular person's behavior because it "doesn't make sense," or it is "unfair." Although you can reason with a person to some extent, emotions are extremely powerful influences. We have found that many highly rational and intelligent people attempt to solve relationship problems using their finely honed intellec-

tual skills. Some people feel that a Talmudic-style logical debate will convince their spouse about one thing or another,
as if they are married to Abaya or Rava (famous rabbis of the
Talmud who engaged in spirited dialogue)! It may be more appropriate to use an emotional response to answer an emotional problem, not an intellectual discourse. In such instances
where the emotional realities are neglected, the end result is
one party feeling that the other is being "silly, immature, or
irrational," and the other party feels frustrated, misunderstood,
foolish, and neglected.

To illustrate the basic truth of this principle, we offer an
example that even the most cerebral and rational readers will
concede to. Should a child be scared of the dark, most people
will not attempt to prove that monsters do not exist as the
principal means to ease that child's fear. Instead, the child will
be given tucks, hugs, bedtime stories, and other forms of
nurture to ease his anxiety and help him go to sleep. This is
because most people accept the fact that children have not
developed their intellectual faculties to the extent that their
fears can be reasoned away. However, even with adults, many
emotional responses know no age, as the case study below
will show.

CASE STUDY:

Leah wants to buy a brand-new dining-room set to host a
large number of guests. Michael simply cannot understand
Leah's "crazy" need for a new dining-room set. First of all,
they cannot afford the one she wants. Second, they have
many other household items to take care of, such as repair-
ing the leaky roof and weatherproofing the attic. Michael can
try to reason with Leah and persuade her that she is wrong.
If that works, fine. However, sometimes a person will not
be persuaded. For example, Leah may respond, "We have a
little extra money saved; why can't we use that?" Michael

may try to point out that they agreed to save that money for emergencies, but to Leah, Michael seems to be overly cautious and miserly.

Michael might be able to "win" this argument from a logical standpoint, but what has he really won? At best, he will have a few more dollars and a disappointed wife. If Michael cannot join with his wife emotionally, in the long run, he is the loser. Michael should consider that if Leah's argument does not make sense intellectually, it might make sense *emotionally*. Michael should ask without sarcasm and in a genuinely curious manner, "Leah, it must be that having a dining-room set is very important to you. Can you share with me more of your feelings about this?" Michael may be surprised to find how much emotional meaning can be attached to an object. In fact, if Michael was honest with himself, he may find that he too attaches "irrational" emotional meaning to objects. He may choose items that are more socially acceptable for men, for example, a certain kind of car, or not having dents in the car, or a kind of suit, or even a religious article such as a *mehudar* tallis or *esrog*. (Some might argue with us regarding the latter examples, because they are religious articles and therefore more justified to spend money on. To this we respond with some poetic license that a house also can be viewed as a religious article for an *aishes chayil* (Jewish term for "an accomplished woman")).

We are not suggesting Michael should agree to buy the dining-room set and bring about their financial ruin. Ultimately, in deciding what to do, it is prudent to use logic, not raw emotion. Nevertheless, the emotional value should not be ignored and must be factored into the pros and cons that go into making the decision. Perhaps, it *would* be worth some financial hardship for Michael, if this allows Leah the satisfaction and pleasure of having a beautiful home. In any case, Leah will feel much better with whatever decision they jointly make, because her feelings were not ignored and her needs were not trivialized.

A LITTLE KNOWLEDGE IS DANGEROUS:

A reader like Michael in the case study above, due to his habitual intellectualizing, might misinterpret and misapply the principles above. After having been sensitized to the underlying emotional and psychological reasons behind Leah's need for a new dining-room set, he may use his cognitive and analytic abilities to convince Leah that he is right. He may think that he is being helpful, by "educating" Leah and interpreting her behavior. He might say something like, "You have attached a certain emotional importance to this dining-room set because it enhances your self-esteem as a hostess, but you should see things from a rational perspective, as you know we cannot afford it right now." While this may be better than totally ignoring Leah's needs, it is patronizing because Michael is not truly *joining* or empathizing with Leah; he is just diagnosing her behavior.

Freud once compared trying to solve an emotional need with an intellectual response to handing out menus to starving people during a famine. Obviously, the people do not need to be told what foods to order to satisfy their hunger; they just need to be fed! So too, in our case study, Leah does not need intellectual insight; rather, she is hungry for emotional nourishment. Unless Michael can learn to genuinely empathize with Leah's need for a new dining-room set, and show a *true* emotional response to this, both Leah and Michael will be left unsatisfied. Michael will continue to be confused and frustrated with Leah's apparent irrationality, and Leah will feel isolated and neglected by Michael's inability to understand and care about her needs.

CONCLUDING THOUGHTS:

Though keen intelligence is a wonderful tool, it is not the most useful skill in interpersonal relationships. A person can excel cognitively and professionally, but unless he or she is able to communicate and respond emotionally to people, his or her relationships will be disastrous. As a final thought, perhaps this is one aspect of what *Chazal* were referring to when they said, "People whose intelligence exceeds their character are compared to a tree whose branches are larger than its roots" (*Avos* 3:13). The end result, of course, is that the tree will fall.

8

ॐ

How to Change
Your Spouse

Over the past few months, we have been getting feedback
from people who say, "Your articles are really interesting, but
I only wish my spouse would read them!" It can be a frustrating challenge in many relationships, when the other person
appears to have a seemingly obvious flaw that you cannot get
him or her to accept, acknowledge, or agree to change. In
this chapter, we will explore this subject in-depth and discuss
some effective strategies and techniques for promoting change
and growth.

UNLESS YOU ARE MARRIED TO
A "LAMED VAVNICK:..."

Most people are not open to criticisms from others. If your
spouse is the kind of person who is receptive and willing to
hear how he or she can change, consider yourself lucky and
do not waste any more time reading this article. Instead, take

him or her out to dinner and tell your spouse how wonderful he/she is.

Paradoxically, we have observed that the closer the relationship is, the more difficult it is to remain open to criticism. This may be due to a psychological need to remain differentiated and separate from the other. According to some psychological theories, the human personality starts out life completely undifferentiated from the world around it. Over time, the infant's personality begins to coalesce and form itself. In early stages of infancy, the child is fully merged with the mother, not seeing himself as separate. Over time, normal developmental crises cause the child to learn to separate from his mother. For example, when an infant's tummy is full and he no longer wants to nurse, he will turn his head away and push the nipple out of his mouth. (By the way, this may be the reason that shaking one's head is a symbol for "No" in many cultures.) Keep in mind, it is easier to know what you *do not* want than what you want. That is why for many young children, "no" is their favorite word. "No" is their way of developing their fledgling sense of independence and apartness. Especially in close and intimate relationships, there is a fear that the personality will dissolve away and somehow be swallowed up by the other. Hence the need to say "No," never quite leaves a person.

Keeping this principle in mind, the more you can communicate a sense of respect for your spouse's perspective and acknowledge the validity of his or her opinion and behavior, the more likely he/she will be open to hearing yours. Being tactful and considerate is helpful, not just because it is merely polite and engenders goodwill. Actually, when you are tactful and respectful in your criticism, you are delivering a message to the unconscious as well. You are in effect saying, "I am not here to 'steamroll' you into doing things my way. We are separate people, and I want you evaluate and consider this matter for yourself."

CHANGING YOURSELF FIRST:

Many people come to therapy convinced that, "quite obviously", their spouse is the one who has the problems. While on the surface this may be true, often, the path to change may involve the other spouse changing first. This is due to the cyclical and mutually reinforcing patterns that many relationships have. Therefore, as long as one person changes, the pattern is broken and everyone in the family changes. This is best understood by the example below.

THE CASE OF THE MISER AND THE SPENDTHRIFT:

Debby is very careful with the family finances. In her mind, if one does not budget and plan each expense, one should not buy it. Of course, Debby is horrified at even the thought of using credit cards. David has a freer attitude with his money. He takes the long view on things. In his mind, life is short, so why wait to enjoy something? You might as well get it now and pay it out over time. Each year he gets a raise, so he feels there will always be more money to pay off whatever debts he accrues this year.

Debby feels David is *obviously* irresponsible with money. David feels that Debby is *obviously* neurotic and miserly. Whether or not either of them is correct is irrelevant. What they do not realize is that as much as they resent each other's habits and personality, they are mutually dependent on each other to maintain homeostasis and functioning within the relationship. How so? If all the financial decisions where left to Debby, the children would go to school in rags for the first month of the year because they have not yet saved enough money for clothes. If all the financial decisions where left to David, they would probably not be able to save for the bigger things.

Taking into account this principle of homeostasis, one can employ it as a novel and indirect way to effect change. Either David or Debby can challenge and change their spouse by themselves choosing to go in the *opposite* direction than they are ordinarily inclined to do. For instance, if Debby could stomach going on a spending spree, David might suddenly become alarmed and disoriented. Unless he is wantonly self-destructive, instead of joining Debby, he will be forced to assess his finances soberly and develop an aspect of his personality that he has ignored for too long. Likewise, if David, all of a sudden, became miserly, Debby may begin to feel restless. Deep down, she enjoys when David insists on spending money. If not for David, they would *never* go out to eat or splurge on anything. Now if Debby wants to enjoy life, she must begin to learn how to tolerate some amount of financial uncertainty, and she can't blame David either!

This homeostatic quality of relationship problems can be found in almost every area where people find themselves at opposite and seemingly incompatible ends. One parent may feel the other is way too strict, while the other feels his/her spouse is way too lenient. Once again, the strategy for change may involve changing your own behavior. When you disrupt the mutually reinforcing behavior by changing your own patterns, over time it induces your spouse to develop regions and aspects of his/her personality and judgment that he/she has neglected.

A WORD OF CAUTION:

As with all of the interventions and techniques we suggest, they will only work if you carry them out without spite and with a genuine and sincere attitude. These are not mere "tricks." If you change your behavior on the surface, all the while looking over your shoulder to see if your spouse is changing too, it won't work. Rather, you must honestly try a new perspective and attempt to change yourself. In the first example above, Debby must really try to convince herself to be more generous and less financially restricted. Or regarding the other example, if you feel your spouse is too soft and not strict enough with your children, you should genuinely go out of your way to be extra understanding and easygoing with them. Remember, the extent that you can genuinely change your perspective and attitude, will be the extent that you will put the prior system in crisis and promote change and growth in your partner.

9

℘

Boundaries for Healthy Relationships

*T*here is a delightful children's story about a lion in the local zoo that had many friends and admirers. Every day, children and adults from all over would come and visit him. He loved them, and they loved him. Of course, he always regretted that he had to be separated from all his fans by the big, thick bars of the cage. One day, the zookeeper forgot to lock his cage, and the lion joyously leaped out to greet his vistors. Of course, he was expecting a great outpouring of love and affection as he could now be physically united with all his human friends. Unfortunately, he was shocked, saddened, and hurt, as the people ran away from him, scared for their lives. "Wait, wait!" he cried, "It's only me,— your friend, Mr. Lion."

The moral of this story is that though Mr. Lion did indeed have many good friends, they required the safety and guarantee of the cage's boundaries to facilitate the relationship. Once the lion went over this boundary, no one felt safe enough to be close to him.

As psychotherapists, most of the relationship problems that
we see stem from a poor sense of boundaries from either one
or both parties. Each type of relationship has different boundaries that are appropriate, and even within types of relationships, individuals may vary in where they prefer to set their
boundaries. For example, in one family someone might ask
her married sister if she is pregnant, while in another family it
would be considered rude. Though they may vary considerably, *all* relationships have boundaries. The important thing
is for them to be perceived accurately and be respected by the
other.

Additionally, boundaries vary from country to country and
culture to culture. In some European countries, people con-
verse with their faces very close together. When Americans
travel to such countries, they feel like everyone is sticking their
noses in their faces when they talk to them.

WHAT IS A BOUNDARY?

Boundaries mean the borders and limits of how far or how
deep the other may tread into the personal and/or emotional
state of the other. A boundary may be a limit on what you
say, what you ask, what you do, and what you touch. If you
see a friend who looks sad, you probably can ask him what is
troubling him. However, if you see a stranger or someone you
only know peripherally, you would pretend to not notice that
he is upset. On the reverse side of the coin, if you are upset
and a friend asks you what's the matter, you might say, "Well,
I am in a bad mood because I just got a parking ticket." On
the other hand, you might *not* say, "I just got fired from my
job," unless you had the sense that the degree of your friend-
ship and appropriateness of the circumstances could sustain
this interaction.

People who are unable to make this kind of assessment accurately often suffer rejection in social circumstances. You may

know a person who in social situations introduces himself *too* quickly to a stranger and reveals *too* much about himself early on in the conversation. Or maybe this person will ask questions or make comments that others feel are too personal. When such interactions are misjudged, the result is discomfort for everyone.

All relationships have boundaries and people rely on them to know what to do, say, and how to act, although they will vary considerably in degree. Even the most superficial relationship, such as two commuters sharing a bench on a subway car, has its unwritten boundary rules. Smile and nod, but do not make too much conversation. When someone violates the boundary, there is discomfort and a need to create further distance to compensate. In deeper relationships, though the boundaries allow for more personal sharing than between strangers, if one party treads too far over the line, no one feels comfortable.

WHY ARE BOUNDARIES IMPORTANT?

Boundaries allow each person to feel safe and secure within the confined closeness of the relationship. Some psychological theories postulate that in early infancy, the child sees himself and his mother and the entire universe as completely merged with him. He understands no separation. Over time, as the personality develops, the child begins to sense what is outside and what is inside. The infant begins to recognize what is separate from him, as he copes with not having what he wants (e.g., his mother's breast the exact moment when he is hungry). It takes a great deal of effort to form a separate personality, and perhaps there always lurks a primitive fear that our personalities will collapse and dissolve away. On a practical level, most people need a certain amount of personal space and independence to function properly. When boundaries are not respected, whether it is in a parent-child relationship, husband and wife, friends to neighbors, or sibling to sibling,

there will always be a degree of aggression and strife to counterbalance the incursion and territorial violation.

Most people do not realize that the key to connection with
people is having a proper separation. If this separation is not
properly understood or tended to, a relationship cannot continue to grow or maintain itself in a healthy manner.

BOUNDARIES, MARRIAGE, AND OTHER
CLOSE RELATIONSHIPS:

Some people assume that the ideal marriage and loving relationships involve the total merger of two individuals. As it states
in Genesis (2:24): "Therefore, a man shall leave his father and
mother and cling to his wife, and they shall be as one flesh."
Although that particular verse is open to debate about its exact meaning, certainly there is some emphasis on the value
of a husband and wife joining together. However, the best way
to achieve this end result of being united and closely attached
is by both parties having great care and respect for the other's
personal boundaries. This is not just true for husband and wife,
but also friends, siblings, parents, and children. Though many
people may feel that in the closest relationships, such as husband and wife or a parent and a small child, there is no need
for boundaries, this is not true. The boundaries may be different, but they still must be respected in order for the relationship to stay healthy and thrive.

Paradoxically, the closer the relationship, the more firmly
the boundary must be established. A simple example of this
principle in operation can be found when you visit the doctor. Even if your doctor is a close personal friend of yours, if,
while he is performing a physical exam he starts talking to you
about something seriously personal in his life (as opposed to
"small talk"), you would feel very uncomfortable. This is
because the psychological process that enables you to be physically exposed in front of him relies on his assuming a some-

what emotionally distant and impersonal stance. Though a physical exam can be sometimes embarrassing, you tell yourself, "Dr. X is performing the role of a professional and not laughing at me behind my back." However, if Dr. X starts talking about his personal life, it upsets this carefully crafted illusion. The unconscious implication is, if he can think personal thoughts at a time like this, what other thoughts is he having? So the closer you come to a person, the more necessary it is to have boundaries to protect the individual emotionally, and at times, even physically.

Because there is great potential for emotional and physical exploitation in familial relationships, it is especially important to be careful about how much you impose on another relative. For example, since your spouse or your child lives with you and would like to do almost anything you ask, you may be tempted to ask, beg, or coerce him or her to do many different things. Often, this is appropriate and normal within a relationship where you equally help each other. However, if your relative begins to feel that his or her personal boundaries are being overrun by your needs; although you may be able to obtain compliance out of fear or guilt, he or she will become necessarily emotionally distant, in order to preserve his or her own sense of individuality.

SOME EXAMPLES OF BOUNDARY PROBLEMS IN RELATIONSHIPS:

As we have stated earlier, boundaries vary significantly from culture to culture, family to family, and relationship to relationship. The examples we have provided are only an illustration and not a definitive guide. Boundaries, like context and language, grow and develop out of the actual usage and interactions between people. However, just as sometimes the wrong grammar or syntax can be glaringly obvious to those who are paying attention, so too with relationship boundaries.

When there are chronic fights and arguments within families, often the underlying issue is a power struggle for personal space in the face of a perceived or real boundary incursion. For example, if a husband and wife fight about money, part of the problem may be that one person is infringing too far on the other's autonomy and decision making. To be sure, if a family is financially tight, on a general level everyone ought to cooperate in trying to save money. On the other hand, if one spouse gets too closely involved and scrutinizes the other's financial decisions, it may be a boundary violation. Similarly, if a parent is constantly fighting with a child over what he wears, or eats, or what kinds of friends he chooses, this may also be a boundary violation. Though obviously it is the role of a parent to set limits for children in an age-appropriate manner, it is helpful to maintain a healthy respect for each child's personal preferences. Parents should try to dictate issues globally, allowing the child to have some personal space and boundaries in the specifics. For example, a parent might *sparingly* dictate what *kinds* of food, clothes, or friends are forbidden, but should try to leave a relatively broad group for the child to autonomously choose from.

Another boundary that is frequently violated in relationships is in the area of disclosure of personal feelings. Though it is wonderful for people to feel close, sometimes one can be too close. Parents may want to share certain feelings or thoughts with their children to "teach them about life." While often this can be wonderful and instructive, one should evaluate carefully if this is merely a way to vent frustrations to an eager and sympathetic listener, or if it is actually imparting important lessons about the adult world. Children, even older children, should not be burdened with adults' problems. Save your venting for your spouse! And even with a spouse, you should be careful not to become emotionally burdensome. For example, if you suffer from chronic pain, your family need not be aware of this at every moment. Though family relationship boundaries call for sharing of feelings so that individuals can get emotional support, the boundaries still put limits on the extent of sharing that is done. Each individual has an emotional life that is separate from the rest of the family.

CONCLUDING THOUGHTS:

Though every person and every kind of relationship has different levels of boundaries that are subject to change depending on life circumstances, there is always *some* boundary. Boundaries are necessary for people to maintain close relationships, because they provide a certain degree of emotional safety and containment so that both parties can maintain their individuality and separateness within the context of the closeness of the relationship.

All relationships are built on an unwritten contract that there will be a limit and boundary to the extent of the emotional involvement. Even the closest relationships require that certain boundaries be maintained and respected in order for each individual to feel safe enough to stay close. If the boundaries are not respected, there will be aggression and fighting as a way to reinforce whatever boundaries were violated. On the other hand, when each individual feels safe with the other, the relationship will then thrive. This is the paradox of relationships: A healthy sense of separation and respect for the differentness of the other person will allow for a maximum amount of closeness.

10

❧

The Use of Silence

Silence is a powerful tool in human relations. However, most people feel uncomfortable with silence and either consciously or unconsciously avoid it, depriving themselves of its great benefits. Because silence is psychologically so difficult to tolerate, you might not even be aware of the many instances throughout the day where you unnecessarily speak or take an action that interrupted a productive silence. In this article, we will explain in detail the philosophy and psychology of silence, as well as some strategies and examples of how to put silence to work for you.

THE TORAH VIEW ON SILENCE:

There are numerous references in the Torah extolling the virtue of silence. For example, in *Pirkei Avos* it states: "The guardian of wisdom is silence (3:17)", and "I have not found

anything more beneficial for the body than silence (1:17)".
An example from *Tanach* is found in reference to Yaakov
Avinu. One can imagine that when Yaakov discovered that
his daughter, Dinah, had been raped, he must have experienced severe distress. Most people in such circumstances are
compelled to take immediate action. On the other hand, the
Torah clearly points out that "Yaakov remained silent until
they [the *shevatim*] came" (Genesis 34:5). This is not to be
compared to Aharon Hacohen's silence when his sons died.
Regarding Aharon, the Torah uses the word *vayidom* (Leviticus
10:3), which connotes Aharon's unprotesting acquiescence
and acceptance of *Hashem's* judgment. However, the Torah
uses the word *hecherish* (see Genesis *ibid.*) to describe Yaakov's
silence. This same word is used in regard to Avraham's ser-
vant Eliezer, who silently evaluated Rivka's behavior to see
if she would act in a manner that would validate the heavenly signs he prayed for (see *ibid.* 24:21). Apparently, before taking any action, Yaakov sat in contemplative silence
to evaluate and understand what occurred.

In halacha, we also find an expression of the value of
silence. When paying a shivah call, one is forbidden to initiate
a conversation and must wait until the mourner speaks first
(*Shulchan Aruch* Y.D., 376:1). What can we speculate is the
reason for this rule? The answer may be as follows: No one is
comfortable with death, and everyone has an urge to make
small talk and avoid the frightening implications of mortality.
However, it is the mourner who may have the most on his or
her mind, and that takes precedence over our feelings. Perhaps the halacha is trying to ensure that the mourner has the
fullest opportunity to express himself, without having others
influence the agenda or topic of conversation. Yet, unfortunately, it is rare to see this halacha employed in practice; most
people end up speaking to the mourner first. Some people
may be under the impression that it is a mitzvah to make small
talk with the mourner to help cheer him up. Such an idea might
be valid, as long as the mourner *first* invites you to do so. Why

do people have such difficulty tolerating silence? Why is it so rare to find people being comforted by another's presence in utter stillness?

THE PSYCHOLOGICAL VIEW ON SILENCE:

As we have alluded to in other essays, becoming fully aware of our feelings is not always an easy experience. The human mind has built-in protective defenses that keep us from being overwhelmed and distracted by the many thoughts and feelings that are constantly in the background of our awareness. This ability to tune out feelings serves an important purpose. Obviously, there are moments in our lives where functionality is more important than being in touch with feelings. For example, you want your airline pilot to be exceedingly competent and professional in his work—and do *not* want him to be "in touch with his inner child" during critical maneuvers. Nevertheless, as with most defenses, our ability to block out feelings is generally overutilized. When we block out too many feelings, we are less responsive to our own needs as well as the needs of others.

In our interactions with people, countless feelings are being evoked and induced that we are hardly aware of. For example, something the other person said may have made you momentarily feel angry, anxious, guilty, or nervous. Even if the person says nothing, his presence alone may arouse, over the course of a few minutes, many different and alternating feelings, ranging from attraction to repulsion. While you may be skeptical about this, if you pay closer attention, you will be able to become more sensitized to the broad range of thoughts and feelings that are constantly passing through your mind. We rely on the flow of conversation itself to distract us from our own inner thoughts. When there is silence, people become more aware of what they are feeling. That is why most people cannot bear to be in another's presence in total silence. The

popular children's game of Staredown is based on this principle. After only a couple of moments, the unvoiced and mostly
unconscious feelings are so great, that one must burst out in
tension-releasing laughter.

You may be thinking, "Even if all this psychological stuff
about silence is true, of what practical use is it?" The answer
is, if you use silence to induce yourself and others to become
more aware of the unacknowledged feelings during conversa-
tions and other interactions, whatever you *do* say will have a
greater emotional impact and be more productive.

THE USE OF SILENCE IN RELATIONSHIPS:

Suppose someone acted toward you improperly or insulted
you. Assuming you have the emotional wherewithal and interpersonal skills to not overreact, you will decide to speak to
that person when the time is right and let him know what he
did wrong in a productive discussion. How you use silence in
this interaction is vital. When you speak to this person, you
might find yourself being overly diplomatic and roundabout
in your complaint, instead of stating your concerns in a direct
manner. This is due to a number of uncomfortable feelings
that you may be experiencing:

1. You may feel vulnerable and worried that your complaint
   will be dismissed or disregarded, thereby potentially adding insult to injury.
2. You may feel uneasy about placing a moral demand on
   this other person because you feel guilty and unworthy,
   or you are afraid that you may have wronged him, too.
   In addition, you may identify with him and therefore not
   want to make him feel bad.

Because of the above dynamics, you will have difficulty stating your complaint and then remaining silent while waiting

for a response. Instead, you might begin to fill in the silence by offering an excuse for him, or make a conciliatory remark such as, "I know I am making a big deal out of this" or "It's OK this time, but please be more careful in the future." When you jump to fill in the silence, you are diluting the strength of your statement. Though it is important to be diplomatic and forgiving, unless it "really isn't a big deal" to you, it is better to save further conciliatory remarks until after the person has had a chance to digest what you are saying and respond to it. Your rebuke would be much more powerful if you state your complaint in one simple terse remark, and then while maintaining eye contact, waited *silently* for a response.

Understand that this has no relation to what people commonly refer to as "The Silent Treatment." We are advocating that you *communicate* your complaint first, and then remain silent. This will allow the full emotional impact of your statement to take effect. What people commonly refer to as "The Silent Treatment", is simply keeping quiet out of protest or anger. People who use "The Silent Treatment" in relationships are harnessing the force of silence to thwart communication instead of to enhance it.

SILENCE IN THE WORK AND BUSINESS WORLD:

The uncomfortable feelings that arise during silence are so powerful, that if you master this method and learn to remain strategically silent, even the most bossy and difficult people can be tamed. For example, if you have a boss who disrespected you, ask to meet with him when he is not busy. In a polite and deferential manner, look him in the eye and tell him in one or two *brief* sentences what he did and how that made you feel. Then keep quiet and wait. Even many of the toughest bosses will cave in and almost slavishly work to "make it up to you."

By the way, this method also works wonders in negotiations. Many stores and firms rely on the consumer's discomfort and feeling sorry for the company or salesperson to limit bargaining. Indeed, if you listen closely, you can notice that some salesmen will strategically leak personal details about their lives to elicit sympathy. For example, a casual remark like "If I go any lower in price, the boss will kill me" may be consciously or unconsciously used to elicit your sympathy. Next time you are bargaining, try stating what price you are ready to pay, and then keep quiet instead of making small talk. If your asking price is reasonable and possible, this trick will make sure you get it.

CONCLUDING THOUGHTS:

The strategic use of silence in conversation causes people to become more aware of what they are feeling. Most people rush to fill in silence with words or action to distract themselves from uncomfortable feelings and thoughts. By resisting the urge to fill in the silence with unnecessary verbiage, whatever you do say will have a greater impact. We conclude with a final word of caution: Silence can be very intimidating, and if you get too proficient in its use, you may be tempted to manipulate and bully people. If you find that people are listening to you without using silence, then as the saying goes, "It's best not to use a hammer to kill a flea."

Parenting

11

꒜

Making the Most out of Playtime with Your Child

 $\mathcal{M}$ any parents see playing games with their children as something they do merely to entertain them. Younger children want you to play *Candyland* with them; older children want you to play *Chess* or *Monopoly*, but it's all the same. Of course, children need attention and enjoy spending time with their parents, and games just happen to be the kind of thing they enjoy doing.

But that is not all there is to it. In fact, playing games with your children, and as a family, can be constructive educationally and emotionally. In this article, we will discuss how you can make the most of this playtime by becoming more aware of the psychology of game playing.

The Jewish tradition has long recognized the importance of games in the lives of children. For example, though running or rushing about is prohibited for adults on the Sabbath because it is not a suitable activity for this holy day of rest, children are allowed to play running games because it is their way of "enjoying the pleasures of the Sabbath." (See *Schulchan Aruch*, O.C., Mishna Bervra 301:2:5.)

WHAT GAMES MEAN TO CHILDREN:

According to some psychological theories, there is a basic human drive to feel competent and achieve mastery over the world. Indeed, echoes of this idea may be seen in the biblical directive to "achieve dominion over the world" (see Genesis 1:28). For children, this need is felt in a most pressing way. Presumably, it is why an infant moves from his comfortable spot on the floor and struggles to walk, despite the repeated painful falls and tumbles he must endure.

Games can be seen as an expression of this need in a more narrowly defined area. Life has countless numbers of rules, and it takes years to attain some knowledge of them. The game universe, however, has fewer and more limited rules. Playing games allows a child an opportunity to practice for the "biggest game of all," otherwise known as life.

Clearly, make-believe games such as house and dress up, are obvious rehearsals for life. But even the notorious and much maligned Cops and Robbers, and its space-age equivalents such as Humans versus the Aliens, are not without a purpose. In fact, they are an effort to grapple with both the destructive and anarchic drives to rebel against authority, as well as the need and desire to conform to the laws of society. Children try on these roles, just as an adult might try on an article of clothing to see how it fits. The child's nascent ego and personality structure oscillates between obedience and rebellion. This can create a great deal of tension, and such games are a healthy outlet for these psychic forces.

A MODEL FOR LIFE:

With this understanding of the symbolic and metaphoric value of games, as a parent, you can teach your child morals and ethics, as well as learn about your child's current views on these matters.

For example, when playing with a small child, does he seek to bend or change the rules in order to win? It is natural for young children to try to "cheat"; they are engaging in an effort to attain competence in any way they can, even if it is not an honest way. What you can do is tap into this need to be competent, and use it to help develop better judgment and reality testing. Follow this procedure:

1. Do not react in an angry or punitive manner.
2. Do not let your child cheat without letting him know you are aware of this, since you will be reenforcing an unrealistic view of the world and negative behavior patterns.
3. Do point out that you are aware that he is changing the rules in order to win.
4. Identify and interpret his behavior so he can learn more about how to manage himself. You might say, "You really want to win, so you are trying to change the rules."
5. Give him a choice about how he would like to proceed. You might say, "I am agreeable to changing the rules to help you win, or I could teach you more about the game so you can win, or I can do both."

An older child may not be motivated to cheat, but may become overly anxious and frustrated if he is losing a game. Instead of calling him a "sore loser" or a "crybaby," the more helpful thing to do, is to identify and reflect back to him his emotional state. This allows him to become more self-aware and make informed choices about how he wants to handle and accept challenges in life. You might say, "I understand that you really wish you can win this game. You feel like a failure and and are angry that you cannot win." Even with an older child, you can then offer to play with a "handicap," such as without a queen in Chess. By discussing this in a straightforward manner, you are showing that, in life, problems can be solved and negotiated in advance, instead of waiting until the level of frustration becomes intolerable.

SOME ADDITIONAL CONSIDERATIONS:

Some parents worry about injuring a child's self-esteem when he is losing, and will make poor moves in the course of a game in order to allow the child to win. This is not the best tactic, since most intelligent children will figure this out. The unconscious message being delivered is, "You are not competent enough to win on your own, and I must protect you." There are no shortcuts for self-esteem; each individual must earn it through personal struggle. You can help your child *attain* self-esteem, but you cannot *give* self-esteem. As we said before, it is preferable to discuss openly how to handicap the game in advance, so both players can play to their full potential. The unconscious message here is subtly, but significantly, different: "You are not competent enough right now to play against me. But I enjoy playing with you and want to teach you how to play at your best so you can learn how to improve your skills."

By applying the above methods, you can help your child become more confident and competent in the world, as he masters his impulses in order to follow the rules, and takes on progressively greater challenges in all areas of life.

12

ॐ

Whining Versus
Expressing Feelings

*I*n our experience, there are two kinds of families that are exceptionally susceptible to emotional trouble and turmoil. The first is the family that has many unwritten and restrictive rules about feelings, the main one being that feelings must be kept under tight wraps and must not be expressed under any circumstances. This family's philosophy is to maintain respect and order in the home by not allowing complaints or whining of any kind. Such rules about feelings may be well founded, as many people have difficulty expressing feelings without being rude, unpleasant, and disrespectful. The second kind of family places no limits on when, where, and how feelings are expressed; there is the sense that "anything goes." The philosophy of these families is to avoid repressing feelings out of a concern that it can somehow be harmful to one's mental health to "bottle it up inside."

Both of these family philosophies have the best of intentions, but at the same time, lose out on the benefits that come from being able to differentiate between children whining and allowing children to express feelings in each life situation. The first family suffers from the stress of repressed feelings, the second family suffers from emotional chaos and lack of discipline.

THE PSYCHOLOGICAL PARAMETERS OF WHINING:

Whining can be defined as expressing oneself in a manner that addresses one's own needs, but does not take into account the needs and feelings of the person being whined at. The Jewish term for this is *kvetching*. In fact, whining shuts out the other person, and at times, can be used as an attack by provoking guilt. On the other hand, expressing even negative feelings can be constructive if the person is open to hearing the other's point of view and speaks in a way that invites the other into honest conversation. We will give some examples of this later on.

FEELINGS HAVE A TENDENCY TO COME OUT, ONE WAY OR ANOTHER:

Later on in this book, we will discuss the psychological, Jewish traditional, as well as common sense perspectives that indicate the value of expressing feelings. Keeping feelings inside or repressed often leads to acting them out in less constructive ways. For example, Danny is jealous of his sister Sarah. She seems to always get most of their parents' attention. Danny does not feel that he can share these feelings, perhaps he knows that his parents would not be receptive to hearing them. Danny may begin to act out his jealousy and need for attention by bullying Sarah, being late for school, or getting "sick" in order to attract more attention. He may even "accidentally" break a window, or slip and fall. This kind of acting out is often not planned in a conscious way. However, people will naturally try to get their needs met in any way that works. In this case, Danny needs the attention of his parents. Teaching children to express feelings, rather than "bottling" them up, has a definite practical benefit for parents. This is because when feelings are expressed, much of their emotional energy is discharged via words and the comforting acceptance of the listener. This eliminates the need to act them out in more insidious ways.

In order to encourage proper character development as well as emotional growth, parents should teach their children the difference between whining and expressing feelings. In the examples below, we will demonstrate how the subtle differences between whining and expressing feelings can either hurt or help people in their relationships.

Example # 1:

Leah does not like the supper her mother cooked today. The first kind of family mentioned above would not allow for Leah to verbalize her discontent, causing Leah to feel resentful, having to conceal her displeasure. If she tries to complain, she will be told, "Do not be disrespectful toward your mother." In the second kind of family, Leah feels free to mutter "yuck" and whine, stating that she "never" gets the foods she likes. This kind of whining helps Leah get her resentment off her chest, but does not take into account the efforts her mother has made in cooking supper for her family in the first place. Leah's whining causes her mother to feel powerless and perhaps guilty for failing to please her daughter. Her mother feels unappreciated, and Leah does not develop good manners.

Example #2:

David is on a car trip to the zoo with his parents and siblings. He would rather be going to a football game and announces this loudly to the rest of the family. David's parents feel deflated after all that went into planning this day. His siblings either agree with David silently, or resent him for putting a damper on their trip. David's whining does not encourage a sympathetic response, so he complains even more. On this day spent together, the whole family ends up feeling apart instead of closer.

Children can be taught to express feelings in a respectful and nonoffensive way, in order to be understood and get their needs met.

GETTING WHAT WE WANT WITHOUT HURTING OTHERS:

It is beneficial for all parties involved to learn how to share feelings without hurting another in the process. As in the first example, if Leah would first acknowledge her mother's efforts to cook after a hectic day, and then state her request for other kinds of foods, her mother would be more likely to want to accommodate Leah the next time. This kind of exchange allows both Leah and her mother to feel heard and understood. Even if Mom does not choose to cook different food for Leah, at least the feelings were discharged in a constructive manner.

In the second example, David can be asked to retrace his steps. He can be instructed to acknowledge his parents' efforts in planning the trip to the zoo, and then respectfully state his preference for the football game.

Of course, the ultimate goal is for children to do this without prompting, but with consistent practice, they can develop the sensitivity to think of others even while trying to satisfy their own needs.

Additionally, this method allows a child the opportunity to develop the valuable lifeskill of optimism. Studies have shown that optimists are less likely to become depressed. Leah's mother's food can't be all that bad, and a child can still be thankful and appreciative. Though children should not be taught to totally whitewash and ignore feelings of discontent, in order to become successful adults they must *learn* to accept situations and even think optimistically. Being allowed to whine without considering another's efforts will not develop this skill.

ADULT DIMENSIONS OF WHINING:

Whining to Your Children:

Sometimes parents vent personal frustrations or feelings to their children, in a desperate effort to be heard and understood by someone, (or anyone!) who will listen. For example, Mom is exhausted from her infant's constant crying, or Dad is upset about a hard day at work. It is not constructive for children to be subject to their parents' whining, nor is it truly helpful to the parent to have a child play the role of the parent's confidante. While it may be tempting for a parent to have the need to be listened to instantly gratified (in this case by one's children), it is not a child's place to fill the emotional needs of adults. A child who is faced with an adult who is venting about adult problems, will have his emotional security threatened. Perhaps he/she will feel frightened by the intensity of the adult's feelings. Or a child may feel obligated to help, but at a loss as to how to "fix" the problem. Children need to know that the adults who care for them are in control, and do not need them to fulfill the role of a spouse or friend. Parents who are able to wait until a spouse or other adult is available to lend a listening ear, will benefit from the real emotional catharsis that is sought, and not have to be concerned that the other person's psychological development will be hampered in any way. Families that have long-standing emotional neglect between spouses, and single-parent families, are more susceptible to this psychological dynamic. This is because someone who has problems in his relationships with his spouse or friends will be more tempted to burden his problems onto the sympathetic ears of his child. This dynamic is known as the "parentified child syndrome," because the child is forced into an inappropriately mature or "parentified" role in the family.

WHINING BETWEEN SPOUSES:

Spouses who whine are caught in a cycle of not having needs met, while simultaneously making each other feel inadequate. As we have stated earlier, whining shuts the other person out emotionally, by depriving him/her of the opportunity to share his/her own feelings and opinions. It is a rare spouse who can respond kindly to a whiner. However, if feelings are expressed in a way that invites the other into open discussion, both spouses will feel heard and understood. Allowing room for someone else when sharing feelings, helps people make positive changes toward getting their needs met. This is because anyone who feels he is being listened to can afford emotionally to listen back. For example, Rachel is upset about Jack never remembering her birthday. Rachel can accuse Jack of not loving her enough and demand a celebration for this year's birthday, or she can verbally acknowledge his commitment to her by saying, "Of course you have shown me over the years how you care for me, but it would make me very happy if you remembered my birthday in some way this year." Jack feels appreciated for his past caring, and is therefore interested in seeing how else he can please his wife. In this way, Rachel is drawing Jack closer, rather than pushing him away.

WHINING VERSUS ACTION:

One school of psychoanalytic thought emphasizes the difference between whining and feeling sorry for yourself as compared with talking about your feelings as a means to direct you toward action. It is important to become aware of and express your feelings. However, some people remain in therapy for years with virtually no emotional growth. In effect, they are paying a therapist to hear them whine. On the other hand, a person can become more aware and in touch with his feelings by talking about and exploring them. After a point though, this should serve as a vehicle to compel him to take constructive action.

CONCLUDING THOUGHTS:

Sharing one's feelings, whether positive or negative, can be an impetus for growth in all relationships. However, some people are taught either to never express feelings, or to selfishly dump all their feelings on others. Withholding expression of feelings in families keeps relationships frozen and discourages growth. On the other hand, whining or kvetching to loved ones does not yield good results, and only causes resentment. Constructive expression of feelings involves educating others about one's self, while inviting the other person to equally share his point of view. Parents can teach this to their children. In addition, spouses who are able to share their feelings as opposed to whining at them, serve as role models for their children. Such children will develop more effective social skills, and be able to get their emotional and relationship needs met more easily.

13

࿇

Using Halachic Obligations to Promote Maturity and Character Development in Children

One of the central tasks of parenting is setting limits for our children. The healthy development of a child's character depends on his learning responsibility and consequences for his actions at an age-appropriate level. In psychological terms, this component of the personality is conceptualized as the "ego," whose role is to mediate between the inner and outer realities.

For example, your inner reality might be telling you that you are late for work and you must get to your destination now! The outer reality might be that it is dangerous to speed and drive recklessly. In this situation, there is a conflict between two realities. A well-functioning ego mediates and manages this conflict. The ego applies objective reason and logic to the situation, and based on past learned experiences, may strategize how to still get to your destination on time. The ego may look for shortcuts, decide to speed up a little but not too much, listen to the traffic report, and so forth. A poorly functioning ego will have difficulty handling the stress of this internal con-

flict between wanting to be at work on time and needing
to preserve one's life. This can manifest itself by erratic
behavior, such as alternately speeding up and then slowing
down (due to the two polar forces that are in conflict), being
impatient and irritable, and in general using poor judgment.

Appropriately administered rules and limit setting with children is the way in which they develop healthy ego functioning, or in layman's terms, responsibility and good judgment.

But what is the best way to teach our children about rules?
This is an especially important question in an Orthodox home,
where aside from the regular rules that all children must learn,
there are several additional Torah prohibitions. Obviously, our
goal is not only to have our children follow the rules, but to
understand and respect them.

When setting limits and rules with children, it is helpful to
maintain an air of firm neutrality. What we mean by this is
being authoritative when setting limits, but not overly invested.
This approach minimizes the likelihood of a power struggle
and tantrum by directing the energy away from personal
emotions, and maximizes the likelihood that your child will
internalize the rule as his own, instead of merely obeying
robotically. For example, if Sarah is banging her doll on the
floor, the wrong way to discipline her is to say harshly or
angrily, "You are not allowed to bang the doll!" The right way
is to state calmly, but firmly: "Dolls are not meant to be banged
on the floor. Dolls that are banged on the floor will break." If
Sarah persists, Mom can repeat herself and add, "If you continue to bang the doll, I will have to take it away." Why is the
second way so much better? Instead of merely imposing a rule
based on the force of your personality, you are educating your
child about what will happen and why she should not bang
the doll. Furthermore, instead of the rule being something that
you made up and she can resent, you are stating it as a fact in
the real world, that is, the doll will break if it is mistreated. In
addition, all humans have a drive to feel independent and competent in their environment. If someone is forced to follow a

rule, he does not experience a direct sense of mastery. However, if one is informed of a rule, he has an opportunity to decide to follow this rule and internalize it.

Of course, a child may still not want to follow the rule, and you might have to take away the doll. Nevertheless, if you act in a firm but neutral manner instead of an angry manner, your child will accept this as a consequence of his behavior, and not a personal issue between you and him. This allows him a chance to independently consider following the rule for the next time.

If you master the above technique (which admittedly has many nuances that take forethought and practice), you will find disciplining your children to be much easier and less stressful for the both of you. The problem with this technique is that even though a neutral and firm tone is always best, sometimes it can be extremely challenging to remain neutral in many areas of discipline. Try telling your son calmly, "Walls are not for writing on," as he crayons up your newly painted living room! (If you are able to do so, you will have done yourself and him a great service. But read on, for a way to train yourself in less stressful situations.)

Through the richness of our tradition, halachic restrictions lend themselves more easily to neutrality because, in essence, it truly is not personal. This is because the religious person feels that both he and his child are obligated in the Torah as a matter of fact, not as a matter of preference. Therefore, such people are afforded the opportunity to use age-appropriate halachic restrictions to develop good habits and judgment in their children. Most people feel bad for a child when he must suffer a halachic restriction that he/she does not understand, for example, not playing with a certain toy that is *muktza* on *Shabbos*. Many parents have difficulty deciding when it is the right age to prohibit a particular activity. Some may feel that it is unfair to impose a restriction that a child cannot yet understand. But actually, enforced in the correct manner, a halachic restriction is a learning opportunity. When, as per your rabbi and custom, you determine that your are obligated to introduce to your child a new religious prohibition, you can use the methods described in this article to teach your child in the most psychologically beneficial manner.

For example, suppose you have decided that it is time for Shaya to learn about waiting the full interval between milk and meat. If you say, "You are not allowed to eat dairy now," you are making it a personal matter between you and your child, that is, he can't eat dairy because you said so. Shaya must then surrender his independence to his mother and father and obey them. He may choose to obey, or he may choose to have a tantrum. On the other hand, if you state, "I know that you would like to eat ice cream now, but the Torah says we cannot eat milk after meat," you will accomplish four positive things:

1. Teach Shaya about the mitzvah, instead of just demanding rote compliance.
2. Show Shaya that you understand and feel compassion for his not being able to eat, which is always good "emotional hygiene."
3. Teach Shaya that one can feel like doing one thing, but still decide to do another (building ego function).
4. Allow Shaya to internalize the rule, instead of merely learning to follow orders.

The benefits of using this method are short-term and long-term. In the short-term, you have a chance to teach your child good habits and discipline in a way that taps into his or her strengths as a person, while deflecting and minimizing interpersonal conflict. In the long-term, your child will internalize the important rules of life and develop good judgment. Children with those qualities are more able to delay gratification, resist peer pressure, and, in general, grow into successful adults.

14

◖

Teens and the Torah Home

*T*he effective parenting of teenagers requires the compassion of Aaron and the zealotry of Pinchas. Patience, flexibility, and good judgment are the tools that will preserve yours and your teenagers' sanity. If you are in conflict with your teenager about whether he or she should be allowed to dress a certain way, go to a certain place, associate with certain friends, you are not alone.

With respect to teenagers and values, the Orthodox home in some ways has it more difficult and in some ways has it easier. It is easier because there is the presumption, which in most cases is true, that the level of trouble and mischief that a religious person can get into tends to be somewhat less severe. On the other hand, it is more difficult for religious parents because the standards of a Torah home can be in daily conflict with the much freer attitudes of the world at large. When your children are small, it is easier to control their access to the secular world, and to filter out influences that you deem harmful. As your children get older, it is more difficult to control their access to those influences. Furthermore, to an extent, it may be appropriate and advisable to increase a child's exposure to secular values, because otherwise, how will they learn to exercise good judgment as adults? (We have come across individuals in treatment, who after being brought up with so many rigid and strict controls, became like "kids in a candy factory" driven to harmful excesses once they have gained adult independence.)

As is well known, adolescents are not full-fledged adults and are not children either. What is not well known is how to treat someone, who at any given moment, can be either, both, or neither! While there are no easy answers, we have put together some useful guidelines, based on sound psychological principles.

LOSE THE BATTLE BUT WIN THE WAR:

Adolescents yearn to be treated as adults and have independence. This is a natural inclination, and should be respected. Even when it comes to matters of religion that you object to, one rarely gives unsolicited advice to friends and acquaintances. On the other hand, it is your job as a parent to direct your children morally and to set appropriate limits. In terms of when and about what you should object to in your teenager's behavior, you should imagine your teenagers as at the midway point on a continuum between young children and acquaintances. In other words, let some things slide. Save your objections for the really big items.

LOOK AT RELIGIOUS ISSUES WITHIN THE CONTEXT OF THE FAMILY'S ACTUAL PRACTICES, AND NOT WHAT YOU WISH THEY WOULD BE:

People often make the mistake of projecting onto their children the values and standards that they themselves do not keep.

While on one hand, it is praiseworthy to try to elevate your children to a higher level of observance than you are able to manage, in reality, as your children become older and develop critical thinking, they will see this as hypocritical. Of course you can always encourage higher standards of behavior, but to mandate it can backfire by corroding trust and respect.

For example, consider the case of a father who expects his son to commit several hours a day to Torah study during the summer, when he himself does not even do his *daf yomi* regularly. While Dad may understandably have many responsibilities that preclude his keeping a regular *seder*, he should not be too surprised to find out that his son does not feel learning to be a priority! Similarly, if you are concerned that your daughter has taken too much of an interest in clothes, makeup, and fashion, before you go to war over this, take an objective look at your own personal values and styles. Some mothers may object, "True, I dress stylishly and enjoy trendy clothes, but what my daughter has chosen is way, way too much!" That may be so, and Mom, it is your job to guide your daughter. Just proceed with sensitivity and an open mind, because what you call "too much" may be in your daughter's eyes, no more or less acceptably *tznius* than the stylish clothes you choose to wear!

CREATE AN ENVIRONMENT OF OPEN, RESPECTFUL COMMUNICATION:

According to Torah values, no matter how old a child is, he must still treat his parents with total respect. However, as a parent, one can set a tone in the house where your children are encouraged to share their subjective complaints in a respectful manner. Everyone makes mistakes. As parents, in the service of preserving a good relationship with your children, it is worthwhile to be open to hearing about them.

This is not to be confused with allowing your child to treat you as an equal. You are giving him the opportunity to express his concerns and to have input, you are not giving up your authority as parent to make the final decision. This can be compared to the Talmudic dictum forbidding a father from implementing corporal punishment on his "older son." The Talmud considers it to be a violation of *Lifnei Iver* (encouraging someone to sin), because such behavior tempts the son to hit his father back. To counterbalance this authority and power given to them, parents are strictly forbidden to be overbearing upon their children. The Talmud (*Moed Katan* 17a) states: "One who administers corporal punishment to his older son should be excommunicated." The Talmud considers this to be an unfair "entrapment," because such parental behavior tempts the son to hit his father back. The Talmud is not saying that a son is justified in hitting his father back. However, at the same time, the Talmud expects the father to exercise his authority appropriately and not to treat his child in a way that will encourage rebellion. The Talmud was only giving one example, and the application of this principle will vary, depending on the current social expectations and what behavior and what age will lead to rebellion. Indeed, Maimonides codifies this principle more broadly. He states (*Yad, Laws of Rebellion* [*Mamerim*], 6:8): "Even though we are thus commanded [to honor parents] it is forbidden to make a heavy burden on one's children or to be exacting in maintaining his honor so as not to cause them to stumble [sin], rather he should be forgiving, as is his prerogative."

DO NOT PERSONALIZE OFFENSIVE BEHAVIOR:

To some extent, teens can be obnoxious. Though they should be reminded to be polite and respectful, do not take their behavior personally. One of the biggest mistakes parents of teenagers make is underestimating their children's growing sense of self and personal pride. An angry and strict tone that once prompted immediate obedience when your child was younger, may in fact, invite a hostile confrontation. It is far more productive to wait for a different and calmer time to point out, in a neutral tone, the correct manner in which you expect to be treated. As we have pointed out elsewhere, in relationships, timing is everything, and this has long been recognized in the Jewish tradition. As we have stated earlier in this book, one might compare this, in concept, to the rabbinic dictum in *The Chapters of our Fathers* (4:18)—"Do not ask forgiveness from someone while they are still angry." The implication of this being, there are definitely better or worse times to work on solving disagreements.

15

≥

Working with Conflicts about Religious Matters between Husband and Wife

*W*hen healthy couples have disagreements in matters of personal preference, or even matters of general values and morals, there is always room for some compromise. However, what if the disagreement is over a halachic matter? A religious person will not find it possible to compromise on what he or she believes to be a major halachic obligation! So what is a person supposed to do? As it says in the Talmud (*Kesubos* 72a,) "*Ein adom dar im nachash bekefifa.*" (One cannot live with a snake in the same wicker basket!) Which means, as important as it is to preserve families, no one is expected to live in an intolerable marital situation.

When a couple steadfastly disagrees on a major halachic issue, it may seem at first to be completely unsolvable. Fortunately though, most of the time, it can in fact be solved. This is because essentially, most people can come to respect another person's religious convictions and want to be accommodating. What usually goes wrong is that the issue takes on a symbolic meaning to one or both parties, making it difficult for either person to feel satisfied, since the underlying issue is not being addressed. There may also be a lack of goodwill and cooperation, stemming from past interactions. We will explain more about this in detail as we elaborate on some examples later on in this chapter. However, before we do this, it is beneficial to keep in mind aspects of what we call "relationship hygiene."

RELATIONSHIP HYGIENE:

Good relationship hygiene, like physical hygiene, means taking steps or preventative care that reduces the chance of health problems arising. If you follow certain "hygienic" practices in your relationship, then you may avoid conflicts such as this from getting out of hand.

The first and most important rule in any disagreement, is to stay calm and to discuss the matter in an open and cooperative fashion. It is a well-known Torah requirement to rebuke a stranger in a gentle and respectful manner (see Maimonides, *Yad, Deos*, 6:6). Surely, one must take even greater care with his or her own spouse! Often, a tactful approach is all that is required to defuse a hostile situation into a completely solvable situation.

Perhaps you are afraid that if you are agreeable and cooperative about a religious matter, it means you are endorsing what you think is sinful. Actually, that does not have to be the case. Being open and cooperative does not mean you have to agree or condone your spouse's opinion or actions; it just means you should show you are listening, and you understand the feelings and thoughts behind your spouse's decision. Showing that you understand another person's viewpoint is not the same as being understanding. Rather, it just shows that there is communication going on, and if you disagree, it is based on having considered the matter fully. This alone, can be a great source of comfort to the other person, as he or she will come to realize that your opinion is not arbitrary. Or, it might even cause you to reconsider your opinion, after seeing merit in the other person's argument.

It is also important that married couples choose a personal rabbi whom both spouses equally trust and respect. It is best to set this up before you are fighting. In this area, there ought to be room for compromise, since there are enough qualified rabbis to choose from. (If as a man, you have a rebbe or *rosh yeshiva* that you feel you must follow, and your wife for whatever reason, does not feel trusting of him, perhaps resolving this issue should be the first piece of marital guidance that you can get from him!)

Finally, consider very carefully the motivations behind your adherence to a particular halachic rule. For example, if you feel obligated to follow a certain *chumrah* (stringency), reasonable and praiseworthy as it may be, is it worth causing marital strife? In addition, does this *chumrah*, which is causing your spouse distress, match your general level of religiosity? For example, does it make sense to abstain from eating *chodosh* ("new" wheat) if you eat Entenmann's and Carvel (*cholov stam*)? Or, if you want to avoid talking idle chatter on *Shabbos*, are you careful with more severe restrictions of speech such as *loshon hora* and *onaas devarim*? Your spouse will be much more willing to respect your religious convictions if they are consistent!

If working with these general principles of relationship hygiene are not able to smooth out your disagreement, then you should consider what the emotional meaning of the disagreement is. Knowing what some of the underlying issues are, may open up doors to compromise that might not be otherwise seen. At the very least, this process will reduce the level of stress and tension between both of you, since you will understand each other's point of view. Let us focus on understanding the underlying psychological dynamics of such conflicts should they unfortunately occur, by analyzing some case studies.

Any relation or resemblance to actual people or families is truly coincidental. All case studies are of a fictional and hypothetical nature. We do not merely change names to "protect the innocent"; we believe the Orthodox world is too small to adequately protect anonymity.

In addition, we chose relatively "bland" disagreements so that the content would be suitable for family reading. However, even conflicts about more serious marital and religious issues operate under the same underlying dynamics, allowing the wise reader to extrapolate further.

CASE STUDIES:

Case Study #1:

Reuven often refuses to go to minyan for *shacharis*. This causes Malkie great distress. She finds this to be incompatible with the standards of a Torah home. Reuven finds Malkie's insistence that he go to minyan to be intrusive and nagging.

In order to resolve this dispute, Malkie might try clarifying for herself what "standards of a Torah home" means to her in a more precise manner. Is she worried about the *chinuch* of her children? Is she worried that she will be embarrassed in front of friends or family if people find out? If Malkie would explain neutrally what her underlying concerns are, perhaps Reuven would agree with her, instead of perceiving her as nagging and "butting into his business."

On the other hand, Reuven might try to clarify what his objections are. Does he feel too overloaded and busy with work and/or personal responsibilities? Has prayer, in some way, lost its meaning? Reuven can then share these concerns with Malkie and they can work together at resolving them.

There may be no simple answers here, but it is important for Malkie and Reuven to realize that this is not solely a *yetzer hora/yetzer tov* issue. There are also other emotional factors, and as a husband and wife, they need to pay more attention to them if they plan to go on living together in harmony.

Case Study #2:

Rena likes to go out once in a while and see a movie. Yaakov does not think it's proper, from a religious perspective, to see movies, due to their secular content. Rena is really frustrated because she starts to feel edgy and restless if she "never gets a chance to go out of the house and do something fun."

Rena needs to clarify if it is a movie in particular that she craves, or just going out. Perhaps she can explore with Yaakov alternate forms of entertainment that they both might enjoy.

On the other hand, if Rena has a real *yetzer horah* to see a movie, she should find out if Yaakov could tolerate her going with a friend instead.

Yaakov might be really upset because his wife is not as religious as he is in this area. He might have an urge to start a big fight about it; after all, he may think: "She is obviously wrong!" While the letter of the law may be on Yaakov's side, Yaakov should carefully analyze his motives. Is he really concerned about his wife's spiritual well-being, or is this more a matter of pride for him? Perhaps this is about his fearing personal embarrassment should people find out about his wife's somewhat irreligious penchant for the cinema. Make no mistake though, even if it is just an "ego" thing for Yaakov, it is still understandable why he is upset. However, if Yaakov wants to increase the chances of his wife responding to his concerns, he should be genuine and honest, and not hide behind a "high-and-mighty" moral stance.

What difference does this approach make? Compare the following two sentences, and see which one you would be more likely to respond to:

1. "You are not acting properly. I can't believe I married someone with such hedonistic tastes. What's so good about a movie? Why watch a bunch of people living and acting immorally?"

2. "Rena, I would like to share with you that your seeing movies is extremely embarrassing for me. I am afraid my *chevrah* at yeshiva will think less of me. I understand that this is something you feel you need, but I want you to hear my side."

Of course, there is no guarantee that Rena will agree, no matter what Yaakov says. Keep in mind, the goal in cases such as this should not be to get your spouse to do exactly what you want. The goal should be to keep discussing the matter in a manner that no one becomes hostile and entrenched in his or her opinions. This way, over time, there is always is a chance for progress and resolution. Meanwhile, there is the intimacy of genuine heartfelt concern, instead of fighting.

As a final word, the case studies above are relatively simple examples and easy to work through. Unfortunately, some couples find themselves hopelessly "gridlocked" on a variety of issues. In such a case, professional help should be sought, in order to improve communication and to correct certain unhealthy underlying foundations in the relationship as well as in the individual personalities.

16

❧

Financial Limitations and Parenting

What do you tell a child who asks for a toy or other item that you cannot afford? Do you make statements like, "Stop whining, you're always asking for new things!" or, "You should be happy with what you have!"? Money problems are a fact of life for most families, and most children will experience not being able to get something, due to their parents' financial limitations. The question is, what is the best way to handle this situation when it occurs.

Because parents desire to fulfill their children's wishes, conflicts can arise when a child's wish does not match financial means. For example, Dovid wants to go to Great Adventure's Theme Park in addition to the safari this Chol Hamoed. Rena would like a new *Shabbos* coat, as the one she has is "out of style." In situations like these, the real problems arise when parents feel guilty for not being able to provide for their child. Sometimes, parents project this guilt onto their children as a way of coping with the financial stress. For example, a child may say, "Mom, I really want to go to sleep-away camp this summer." This particular camp is beyond Mom's financial means. Mom feels guilty, but finds it difficult to share her feelings and the objective truth about the family's financial affairs. So Mom says, "Do you always have to choose the most expensive options with everything?" or "I don't think that camp is for you. I heard XYZ about this camp, I know you won't like it."

The first step in being an effective parent in these situations (as in many others) is to try to understand your own feelings. If you are feeling guilty or inadequate that you cannot fulfill your child's request, it is important to recognize those feelings, and not cover them up by rationalizing different reasons for not doing so. When parents acknowledge limitations in life, it teaches children that not having enough money is not necessarily a weakness. Not having everything in life can be character building, if children are included in the process and not dictated to. Children feel recognized and respected as people if honest explanations are given to them. Children need to know that the reasons you give them are the real ones. This type of honest communication between parents and children fosters greater understanding, closeness, and trust. Of course, as a parent, it is up to you to decide how much is appropriate to share about your financial situation, based on your child's age and developmental level. The main point is to acknowledge their feelings and to avoid criticizing their wishes because of your own feelings of inadequacy.

This kind of honest communication enhances your child's self-esteem as a direct result of acknowledging his wishes as acceptable and legitimate. (Children take cues from their parents as to how they view themselves. If their parents think that their needs are OK, then they view themselves as OK.) In this way, children get the message they are accepted, their wants and dreams are legitimate, and that their parents are interested in hearing and knowing more about them. Additionally, parents can utilize these positive interactions as a way to model for their children how to handle limitations in life.

The next time your child makes a request for something that you cannot afford, take a brief moment to ask yourself how you feel about this fact, and acknowledge these feelings to yourself. Then listen, hear what it is that your child wants, and why it is important to him/her. You may be pleasantly surprised to find that both you and your child feel more closeness, acceptance, and appreciation for each other than before, even though you are unable to fulfill the request!

SAMPLE DIALOGUES:

Getting back to our examples of Dovid's wish to go to the amusement park and Rena's wish for a new coat:

Wrong Way:

"Why do you want to go to the safari? You know the animals come really close, and you can get dirty. And those rides in the park, they're so long. You'll never get to go on the ones you really want anyway!"

"You always choose the most expensive trips!"

Right Way:

"The rides and safari at Great Adventure really do sound exciting. What's your favorite ride? (Listen.) I wish you could go, but we don't have the money right now for such a big trip. Let's talk about what else we can do together that is affordable."

Wrong Way:

"You never seem to be satisfied with the clothes that you have!"

Right Way:

"Did you have a specific style/color in mind? Describe it to me. Oh, so that is what your friends are wearing? We're not able to afford a new coat for you right now, but I know it is important to you. Would you be willing to use some Chanuka/birthday money to help save for it?"

CONCLUDING THOUGHTS:

Remember, discussing your child's wish does not necessitate assuring that the wish comes true. But if guilt or other emotions get in the way, and parents feel that they have to make the wish happen but cannot, then it is difficult to talk about. The opportunity for finding out about your child's ideas and sharing them is lost. Furthermore, when a parent, due to guilt feelings, expresses disapproval when a child is simply making a request, the child feels rejected and gets the message that it is not acceptable to ask for things, or perhaps to even want them!

17

❧

Adjusting to a New Sibling

*H*ave any of your children been acting "babyish?" What possible reasons could there be for infantile behavior in older children? In this chapter, we will suggest one cause for babyish behavior in children, and how to make life easier for parents in these situations.

If a new baby has arrived, or your older child simply never got over the existence of a younger one, he may act out his jealousy by behaving like a baby. The shifting in family placement can be difficult emotionally for parents as well as older siblings. Does this sound familiar? Things seem almost perfect, but then your older child disrupts your special time with the new baby. He is quite annoyed with you for bringing home someone new, but may or may not show his feelings outwardly. "Big" baby may decide to cry more, fall and hurt himself, or refuse to help with chores. Even in families where there is no newborn infant to complicate matters, and all of the children are beginning to mature, sometimes there is one child who continues to whine, tantrum, and behave like he is three or four years younger than his real age.

Older siblings sometimes act out their jealousy over a new baby, or a younger sibling who once was the baby, by suddenly reverting to behaviors that you thought they had long outgrown. When a child feels pressure to grow up, that he is expected to now be a big brother, he may resist and try hard to hold onto being "the baby" in the family. After all, it wasn't his idea to get a new sibling!

On the other hand, as we have mentioned in earlier chapters, under the right conditions, children will take advantage of any opportunity given them to prove their competency and their "bigness." Having contradictory feelings, such as, wanting to be big and little at the same time is normal in both children and adults. If you can plan ways to give your older child a chance to get used to his new situation in life, he will likely learn to enjoy being big, and therefore helpful to you in caring for the baby, or his younger siblings.

GETTING INTO THEIR SHOES:

Parents who allow their child to feel free not to be big, will find that their older child will more readily ease into the big brother/sister role. A child who feels comfortable being the older sibling, will then naturally seek ways to be helpful. For example, little Sarah, age three, is used to having Mommy all to herself when she comes home from nursery school. She gets a snack and a story each afternoon. All of a sudden, one day, Mommy is not available—but worse—she is giving away her love to someone else! Sarah may feel overwhelmed with the loss of her mother's time and attention. She may even think that she has been replaced. Sarah gets an idea. If she could somehow turn herself into a baby, Mommy will definitely return her attention to Sarah, just like before. (*Who knows? Maybe Mommy will even dump the baby out!*) These feelings of anger and sadness will likely cause Sarah to tantrum, whine, and refuse to be helpful. In an effort to help Sarah adjust, Mother or Father may tell her that she "is a big girl now" (and expect Sarah to behave accordingly). While under some circumstances, this may help Sarah feel good about herself, in this new-baby situation, Mother's remark can well have the opposite effect. Sarah will not be receptive to the "big girl" theme. After all, if being a big-girl means not getting special time with Mommy, then why be big? Rather, Sarah may stubbornly retort "I am not big!" She will be difficult at a time when Mother and Father most need all the cooperation they can get.

ADJUSTING TO A NEW SIBLING:

Here are some things to keep in mind to help children of all ages adjust to a new sibling:

1. Warn Sarah in advance that she will not have Mommy all to herself for snack/story time. Children, as well as adults, need advance warning if daily routines will be changed.
2. Acknowledge that baby takes up a lot of Mommy's time, and allow your child a chance to talk about and adjust to this new reality.
3. When practical, offer to treat Sarah "like a baby." For example, cradle her in your arms, or sing a lullaby. Letting Sarah regress at designated times will help her to feel understood, and get "being little" out of her system. She will then be free to move on and grow into being the "older sister."
4. Encourage discussion on how Sarah might wish she was the baby. Do not be concerned that this will cause Sarah to act infantile from now on. Discussion merely allows Sarah to express what was on her mind anyway,

and will help her adjust to being a big sister sooner. This will allow Sarah an opportunity to work through her feelings in a more constructive way. Remember, feelings have a way of coming out, one way or another. As a parent, you want to encourage your child to express feelings instead of acting them out by misbehaving. A child may feel great relief to know that her feelings are acceptable to her parents. Contrary to what many parents believe, simply talking and listening to a child about a problem is often enough to resolve it.

If all of the above points are followed, your child can make a smoother and faster adjustment to the new baby. Your child will hopefully conclude that she can feel more loved by Mommy in "being big" (helpful), than by whining and throwing temper tantrums. She will soon begin to ask if she can help bathe, diaper, and feed the baby, and will enjoy being an older sister.

CONCLUDING THOUGHTS:

When older children are jealous of a younger sibling, they sometimes act out these feelings by behaving like a baby in the hopes that this will get them more love, affection, and attention. This kind of behavior makes life more difficult for parents, who need life to be going relatively smoothly in order to be able to focus on the new baby's needs. Parents can elicit helpfulness from their older children by talking about the changes in their child's life, encouraging expression of all feelings, and providing opportunities for her to be treated "like a baby." These will help your child feel understood, and move her along into the role of the older sibling faster and with less resistance.

18

❧

Good Habits for Back to School Time

$\mathcal{W}$ith the beginning of the new school year, it is a great time to get rid of some bad habits and start some new good ones for yourself and your children. When it comes to younger school-age children, many parents find themselves working harder on their child's homework assignments than he or she ever does! No matter what age, every child should become gradually more independent and responsible. If a child is old enough to receive assignments, he is old enough to take responsibility for them! The difference between a stressed-out parent and a relaxed parent has to do with creating an environment where children are encouraged and empowered to independently manage their affairs.

Can this really work? Yes, it can! It is a basic human drive to be competent and to control your own environment. Children, as they grow, especially need to have this feeling. On their level, they are constantly striving to feel competent. Often, what you mistakenly see as misbehavior, is actually a misdirected effort by your child to fulfill his need to be in control. For example, a daily struggle with a young child over bedtime is actually about him struggling to feel grown up and that he is a master of his environment. Obviously, he is not old enough to unilaterally decide his bedtime; however, you can channel this drive in a way that energizes you and your child.

In the critical areas of homework, bedtime, and wake-up time, your child can and should learn to take responsibility. As a parent, you only have to set up age-appropriate limits, leaving your child with the task of managing his own affairs within these boundaries.

BEDTIME / WAKE-UP TIME:

Some parents are burdened every morning with rousing their children from bed. Many times, this situation worsens with the parent having to come back several times before the child wakes up. Furthermore, you and your child lose out on spending quality time in the morning, with everything being reduced to a tense, last-minute rush.

Your child's bedtime should be determined based on two factors:

1. His ability to remain awake and in a pleasant mood.
2. His ability to wake up independently the next morning.

Within reasonable limits, you should let your child choose a regular bedtime that he must remember to abide by on his own. Inform your child of your expectation that he go to sleep, wake up by himself, and be ready by an agreed-upon time. It is ideal to buy him an alarm clock, so he gets the message that waking up is totally his responsibility. (For children who cannot tell time easily, consider a digital clock.) In addition, you expect your child not to be cranky, and to be helpful around the house when asked. The reason being that a child who is too tired to be helpful and in a good mood is not getting enough sleep.

If he cannot abide by these rules, then you choose an earlier bedtime. You should explain that you must enforce an earlier time not because it is a punishment, but because he was unable to function with the later bedtime. Try moving the time about fifteen minutes earlier, and explain that you will see if he is now able to follow the rules with this earlier time. You can also explain that, if he does well with this bedtime, you will be open to changing to a later time, in a week or so.

You may think your child will be upset just about going to bed earlier. However, what is really upsetting him is his loss of autonomy and control. By making the rules about bedtime dependent on his behavior, you are inviting your child to become competent and in control of his affairs, by controlling his behavior instead of controlling you.

With very young children, who like to be read a story or hugged and tucked in before bedtime, you can still implement this rule. It is just a matter of pointing out that you will spend "tuck-in" time with them as long as they are ready (e.g., having brushed their teeth, changed into pajamas, etc.) and in bed at the agreed-upon time. Once again, within age-appropriate limits, your child is taking responsibility and control of his schedule, freeing you from the burden of reminding and prodding him.

HOMEWORK:

Some parents spend the entire evening nagging their children to do homework. The problem arises from the unfortunate and often accurate perception that the homework is more important to the parent than it is to the child! This dynamic must be changed. The noted child expert, Dr. Haim Ginott, points out that as a parent, you must communicate to your child that homework is a contract between him and his teacher, and not between you and his teacher.

You may wonder, "How is this possible? What if my child does not want to do the work, should I just let him get away with it?" The answer is, of course not. But your fears may be overrated. Once again, normal children will have a drive and desire to feel competent. They will not want to come to class empty-handed. So while your child may need some guidance and structure, he really has a need, for his own reasons, to complete his assignments.

You should sit down and discuss with your child what the evening routine should be. Homework before or after snack? Before or after supper? Then, place a limit on what time the homework should be completed. If it is done by that time, he can go out and play, you will read him a story, and so forth. If he cannot complete his homework by the set time, he will lose the ability to control and determine his own schedule. You will tell him he needs to do his homework right away when he comes home. It is important to show, in your tone and manner, that you are not punishing him. Instead, you are taking responsibility for an area that he is unable to manage at this time. You really want him to be responsible, and you can inform him that in a week or so, you will try again with letting him manage his homework.

If you follow these guidelines, you can create a more pleasant and cooperative environment in your family. It also will help your children develop the necessary skills of self-management that they will have to master to become successful adults.

This article originally appeared in the *Jewish Press* (October 8, 1999). Subsequently, we received the following letter raising an important point that should be clarified:

Dear Feuermans:

Your advice regarding homework makes sense on paper. However, I don't think you realize how some yeshivas load it on. Almost every evening my children come home with an inordinate amount of homework. When you add the long school days, dual Hebrew and secular studies, tests, and reports, you are dealing with a heavy schedule.

As things stand today, how do you really expect these children to "budget their time and manage their homework?" Though in theory your ideas are excellent, in reality you are placing children in a no-win situation.

Our response:

We are assuming the homework assignments themselves are appropriate. In such a case, parents should not get over-involved and should allow children to manage their responsibilities in a fairly autonomous manner. Apparently, the person who wrote this letter feels that the degree and amount of homework assigned by the teachers are too difficult and too numerous. Children have a responsibility to complete their assignments; however, parents and teachers have a responsibility to ensure that the assignments are fair and the environment in which to do them is conducive. If you feel that your child is being assigned too much homework, this is a something that you should take up with your child's school. Since it may be difficult to determine what exactly is the appropriate level, we have listed some general guidelines and suggestions below.

SOME GUIDELINES FOR APPROPRIATE HOMEWORK:

The following guidelines are based on an article written by Mr. Stanley H. Fischman, published in the October 1977 edition of *Machberet Hamenahel: The Yeshiva Educator's Notebook*, edited by Rabbi Chaim Feuerman, EdD., published by the National Conference of Yeshiva Principals affiliated with Torah *Umesorah*.

	Jewish Studies	General Studies
Grade 1	10 minutes	10 minutes
2	15 minutes	15 minutes
3	20 minutes	15 minutes
4–5		Total 45 minutes
6–7–8		Total 1 hour.

Additionally, Fischman recommends that a portion or sample of the homework be done with the children in class, so that the teacher is sure that each child understands how to do it. Furthermore, the function of homework is to review the day's lessons, not to learn new material. If your child does not know enough of the work to complete the homework, something is going wrong with the educational process. For whatever reason, your child is apparently not learning the material well enough in school. In such a case, it is important to have a trouble-shooting conference with the teacher.

ADDITIONAL CONSIDERATIONS FOR PARENTS:

Many children do not have the initiative or skills to make strategic decisions about their assignments. They may waste twenty minutes trying to figure out one question that they do not know, and then find themselves too exhausted for the rest of the assignments. Parents should coach children to skip anything they do not know. Once all the assignments are completed, the child can bring the homework with the unanswered questions to his or her parent. Depending on how much time was already spent and the child's general ability, the parent can then decide whether these questions should now be worked on or left incomplete.

Some children or parents may object to leaving out answers; after all, the child might get a lower mark! This too, is an important lesson for children (and parents!) to learn. Our community has confused the ethic of constant striving for excellence in Torah and mitzvos, with striving for academic excellence. They are not the same. Whether the homework is *limudey kodesh* or general studies, a grade of 100 on an assignment *does not* assure a grade of 100 in Torah and *yiras shamaim*. It is OK to get a B on an assignment, as long as a child is developing his character and his knowledge at an acceptable pace.

CHAPTER

19

❧

Loving an Unlovable Child

$\mathcal{S}$ome readers may find the title of this chapter alone to be disturbing, not to mention the content. Therefore, by way of introduction, we want to clarify what compelled us to write about this topic. A person wrote to us requesting that we write an article on how to love an unlovable child. This person said, "I have come to realize that not all children are naturally lovable, and I would like to know what your view is on this matter." Although this is admittedly an unusual topic, if the person asking indeed feels that his child is unlovable, and is honest and courageous enough to ask the question, he certainly deserves an answer. In addition, perhaps there are other people out there who have had similar feelings and could also benefit.

This question raises many psychological and moral issues, and we are hesitant to state one opinion or offer a neatly packaged solution. Instead, we thought it might be more helpful to share some of the key points that emerged as we discussed this among ourselves:

117

Chaya: I think there are times during a child's life that you just might really hate him or her. But when that happens, it happens. You can't always love a child.

Simcha: Aren't you confusing "hate" with "not loving?" True, a child can be annoying, and you can be angry with him and feel hate, but does that mean you don't love him? Maybe we are not clear on our definitions here. I define love toward a child as providing protection and nurturing, not the kind of yearning to be close that is described regarding romantic love. If you are taking good care of your child, responding to both his physical as well as emotional needs, that's loving him. And, that needs to be done consistently if you want to be an adequate parent.

Chaya: I have no argument with what you are saying. However, my understanding is that the person asking the question is not referring to an inability to act in a loving manner. Rather, he is plagued with guilt because he does not feel love toward his child. Regarding this, of course, it's a bad idea to tell your child you don't love him, but it is not so unusual if you sometimes feel that way. So I would advise the person, "Don't worry and don't feel so guilty, as it is normal and human to sometimes have feelings of dislike toward your child. Just keep your thoughts to yourself, and treat him as best as you can."

Simcha: What if it is not just "sometimes?" What if a person most of the time does not feel love toward his child? Even if a child is incredibly obnoxious, most parents are able to muster sympathetic feelings toward him. For a parent to chronically feel no love toward his or her child, my sense is that such a parent does not feel loved enough himself. I am curious about the intergenerational marital and family issues of the family of origin. Does this parent feel that his parents took good enough care of him? Is there enough emotional satisfaction in his marriage? If someone finds himself consistently unable to love his child, I think he needs to look into his other relationships and work on improving them. This will provide him with the emotional fuel he needs to give love to a very demanding child.

Chaya: Returning to the guilt theme, I wonder if this "lack of parental love" is not stemming from this difficult child constantly making his parent feel like a failure and ineffectual. The lack of love might be a combination of anger at him for not behaving, not doing well in school, not being a source of parental pride, as well as guilt for the parent who has not succeeded in changing him. In other words, this child is a constant thorn in his parent's side. Every time he sees his child underperform, he receives a narcissistic injury and blow to his ego, as he is reminded of his own real, or imagined failings as a parent and as a person.

Simcha: Actually, your interpretation also can answer another question: What if a child is physically malformed or developmentally disabled in some severe way. Though most parents in such situations report that they are able to love their children no matter what, there must be those who do not feel that way. For them, the feelings must be very complicated. First, there might be anger at the child for just existing. As you said, some parents might suffer injury to their pride every time they are reminded of their child who falls below their personal expectations. Second, there must be guilt about feeling this way. In order to avoid being locked into an emotional cycle of anger and guilt, a parent in this situation should be honest with himself about his feelings and come to terms with them. For many parents, it must be disappointing and embarrassing to have a child that is far from the Jewish parent's dream. However, though it is a lot easier said than done, an emotionally mature and developed person does not base his self-esteem on his possessions, nor on his children's achievements.

CONCLUDING THOUGHTS:

In this dialogue we covered the following basic points:

1. Acting loving toward a child is different from feeling love toward him. It is necessary to provide consistent and adequate physical and emotional care for a child, no matter how you may personally feel. If that is done adequately, personal and private feelings about the child may be less significant.
2. Having said that, it is normal to sometimes feel so annoyed and fed up with a child that you do not feel any love toward him or her.
3. If there is a chronic lack of love and animosity toward a child, there may be other underlying issues, such as:
   a. You feel that you did not get enough love from your own parents, or your current adult relationships are not emotionally satisfying enough. You then are too depleted emotionally to give this demanding child what he or she needs.
   b. You take this child's failings personally and see them as a reflection on you. You resent this, and also feel guilty about this. The complexity and conflictual nature of these feelings makes it hard for you to feel love toward him or her.

20

❧

Report Cards
Dos and Don'ts

*F*or many parents and children, report cards bring a great deal of anxiety. When being presented with an unsatisfactory report card, most parents realize that whatever has gone wrong during the semester cannot effectively be addressed in one angry rebuke. However, as with most anxiety, it often causes people to overreact in an irrational manner. Therefore, many parents will find themselves shouting, punishing, and threatening a child who has done poorly. All the while, a little voice in the back of a person's head may tell him this is the wrong thing to do, but at the same time he feels strangely compelled to continue his tirade.

Some parents may overreact to poor report cards because they feel as if they are the ones being graded and they are the ones who have failed. The power of this kind of transference of emotions should not be underestimated. Upon honest reflection and introspection, such parents may even discover feeling the same "butterflies in the stomach" anxiety that they used to get when they, as children, were sent to the principal's office! As parents, in order to free our children to grow, we must let go of the past and resolve our personal issues about past successes and failures.

Furthermore, one psychological theory holds that the primary function of education is to teach children to delay gratification. If you think about it, most scholarship involves learning appropriate rules, processes, and procedures, and when to apply them. This holds true whether the subject is Gemara, grammar, or arithmetic. If, as parents, we jump to an emotional and nonrational response to a report card because of our own fears and failures that it represents, we are modeling behavior that is the exact opposite of how we want our children to behave in order to succeed in school. We want our children to be thoughtful, rational, and to control their urges in order to maintain and preserve an organized environment of learning. When discussing a poor report card, we want to show the same behavior.

Below are some general guidelines of report card "Dos and Don'ts," based (with permission) on a parent handout authored by Rabbi Naftoli H. Basch, *menahel* of Yeshiva Ketana of Queens:

Please realize that a report card is a way of informing a parent of the status of the child's progress to date. It is not a general evaluation of what type of person your child is or what type of parent you are. At times, parents get offended when grades are not up to par. Some may even adopt a position that they must serve as their child's lawyer and challenge certain grades with the school. Others will compare their child's grade with those of his friends, brothers, sisters, or neighbors. This can cause parents to react very harshly toward their child. Of course, this is counterproductive.

Upon reviewing the child's report card, the first and foremost parental responsibility is to discuss it with the child in a nonemotional and nonconfrontational manner. It should be done privately, not in the presence of friends or siblings. The child should immediately be praised for his good grades, and assured that you will help him improve the grades that are not up to par. Of course, he should be asked for his perception as to why certain grades are below expectations. A final decision as to how to go about raising a child's grades should be held off until after the parent/teacher conference.

It is also important that the parent, and rebbe or teacher hear the child's feedback. What does the child feel about his grades? Does he think he can do better or try harder? Of course, a child's perception is not always a true indication of what is happening, but in order to understand the child better, we must attempt to know his feelings. Rebbes and teachers can then work along with the parents in explaining what is expected of the child and giving the encouragement necessary to reach these expectations.

It is very important that the positive aspect of the report be stressed, even in situations where the report card on a whole is not up to par. Parents should also convey to the child that the future is more important than the past, and assure that they will be working with the rebbes and teachers to help improve grades. Although a child should never be rejected due to an unsatisfactory report, still, he must be held accountable if the below-average grade was due to poor behavior or lack of effort. Proper incentives and/or disciplinary measures may be called for. However, these measures should not be a spur of the moment "knee-jerk response." Rather, they should be the products of a thoughtful and rational plan, based on feedback and discussion with all parties involved.

21

᷂

Self-Destructiveness in Children

*I*n the chapter "How to Help Someone Who is Self Destructive" we noted, "Ironically, it is the friends and loved ones who feel the most despair and distress, not the self-destructive person himself. However, since you cannot effectively stop anyone from doing what he really wants to do, you must let go of your guilt and give up control. Obviously, you want to help save this person, but you cannot take upon yourself the impossible burden of trying to keep afloat someone who wants to drown!" We then suggested, "The goal is to help make this person more aware of his unconscious destructive behavior, so he can be free to evaluate it and make better choices. Follow this rule: Never let your level of interest or energy exceed the energy of the person you are helping. If you see that it is, do not get angry or criticize him. Instead, ask in a genuine and curious tone why this appears to be so. Then, be open to his response. Try to engage in a meaningful discussion not based on pressuring him or her to do something, but just on being curious about his or her apparent self-destructiveness."

A schoolteacher responded by asking, "How would you advise applying these suggestions in your article to children? With a self-destructive child it is much harder to remain passive while he engages in harmful behavior. For example, a child with high aptitude who does poorly in school, or a child who seems to unnecessarily alienate his peers and suffers from social isolation?"

This is an excellent question, and clearly a child who is acting in a self-destructive manner requires a different response than an adult. In such a case, more often than not, for a child, the best option is family therapy treatment. A self-help book is insufficient to effect a cure. However, we will provide some basic guidelines to serve as a supplement, not as a substitute, for therapeutic intervention.

As adults, we feel a greater level of responsibility to guard the welfare of children, and thus, even if you, as the adult, are more interested in saving the child than he or she appears to be, it still may be wrong to stand idly by. On the other hand, getting overinvolved in any situation is rarely helpful. And even with a child, it is hard to see how you can help him if he is constantly engaging in behavior that thwarts your attempts. So, what can you do?

HELPING A SELF-DESTRUCTIVE CHILD:

Since a child's personality is not fully formed, much of his behavior is a reflection of the significant adults in his life. In situations such as this, the two key questions to answer are:

1. "Which adult in the child's life is most affected and hurt by this behavior?"
2. "What is this child trying to communicate to this adult by this behavior?"

The child's behavior can improve dramatically by addressing the relationship issues that are brought up by whatever answers these questions yield. As we have stated above, the most effective way to do this is through family therapy.

SPECIAL ADVICE FOR TEACHERS, PRINCIPALS, AND OTHER NONFAMILY CARETAKERS:

As much as you attempt to help a child, be sure that your level of interest or energy does not exceed the level of concern that the parents exert. This is a sign that you are getting overinvolved. Instead of trying to "save" this child all by yourself, you should share your concerns with the parents, in the hopes that they will learn more about whatever disturbing signs and symptoms you are seeing. However, if the parents do not respond to your satisfaction, your further overinvolvement is inappropriate. Obviously, if the child is in some danger, you may need to take action. Otherwise, you should limit your efforts to a level that is matched by the significant others in this child's life.

Please note, whenever you are trying to help anyone who is self-destructive, be it a child or an adult, you can never guarantee that the self-destructive person will change his behavior. This is because whatever psychological issues that are compelling an individual to act in such a manner, and whatever family dynamics contribute to a child's self-destructive behavior, cannot be modified without the person's or the family's total commitment to change. This will be more likely to occur if you realize that you can only take so much responsibility for another's welfare. As our rabbis astutely observed, "It is forbidden to have mercy on a fool (*Sanhedrin* 92a"). If you follow these suggestions, you will be able to minimize your frustrations and maximize whatever benefit and aid you can provide.

22

৵

My Child is Unpopular in School

$\mathcal{F}$or a child or adolescent, being unpopular is emotionally painful. For a parent, it can be a bewildering problem. In such cases, there may be numerous contributing factors that can be difficult to sort out. In this chapter, we will discuss some specific strategies for identifying and remedying this social problem.

(For the purposes of this chapter, we use the term "unpopular" to connote being the brunt of merciless taunts and being socially rejected and isolated, not merely being unpopular.)

EXPLODING THE MYTHS:

Do not assume that external and material causes are the sole basis for unpopularity, such as, blaming it on mean and selfish classmates, or on not having enough money, toys, or clothes. Though these can be contributors, ultimately, it is your child's personality that is the crucial factor in his retaining friendships. If you examine his peers, though the most popular ones in the group may have "cool toys" or stylish clothes, you also will find children who are economically similar to your child, and who are not social pariahs. We are of the opinion that, when it comes to making friends, even a physical handicap or obesity is relatively insignificant in comparison to personality.

Though it may be due to a complicated combination of personality traits, over time, the causes for your child's unpopularity most likely can be uncovered. Once you uncover the causes, hopefully, you can work with your child to correct them.

POTENTIAL PITFALLS:

A potential danger is your becoming overly invested in this issue. If you are honest with yourself, when your child is unpopular, it is also a blow to your own self-esteem. No one wants to think that his child is, in some way, socially inept. If you are not careful, this can cause you to become impatient and critical when discussing this problem with your child. Of course, that will only exacerbate the problem with your child. Aside from his already complex social problems, he is now burdened with pressure from you. Additionally, if he is somewhat rebellious, it will cause him to unconsciously resent you and possibly sabotage your efforts to "help out."

ASSESSING YOUR CHILD:

Being as objective as possible, how does your child's behavior seem to you? Pay attention to his interactions with you as a parent, his siblings, and friends.

(If you have difficulty doing so, a sibling will often have a wealth of information about the negative social behaviors and habits of another sibling. If asked, he may bluntly tell you the exact problem, albeit, with his own biases and rivalries.)

Does your child:

1. Act immature for his age?
2. Have difficulty sharing?
3. Have any annoying habits (e.g., interrupting people, talking too loudly, touching, fidgeting, picking his nose, etc.)?
4. Have a bad temper?
5. Grab toys or become physically aggressive?
6. Have poor hygiene, unusually bad breath, or body odor?

If your child seems to be socially inappropriate in some of these areas, you may be able to help by having an honest discussion and bringing these shortcomings to his attention.

TALKING TO YOUR CHILD:

It is not going to be easy for your child to own up to the fact that he may be pushing away friends and singling himself out for ridicule. Therefore, it is important that you speak about this issue in a manner that allows him to integrate constructive criticisms and observations. If he is going to make any significant changes, he needs you to be clear and honest, and not "sugar coat" the problem. Keep in mind, whatever you say will be far less cruel than what his classmates are saying already! On the other hand, if you overdo it and cause your child to become too defensive to tolerate any criticism, you will end up getting into an argument that you cannot win.

The best procedure is to ask your child open-ended questions that help him draw his own conclusions. It will be much less of a blow to his self-esteem if he can partially realize his shortcomings instead of you just listing them. You might ask him if he has any idea why his peers make fun of him. If he says, "No," or he says, "Because they are all mean," don't let him off the hook so easily. You should tell him, "Though it could be that your classmates are mean, there still may be reasons why they are especially choosing you to be mean to." You should encourage him to think harder. If he still cannot think of anything, ask him if he is open to hearing what you think might be causing it, based on how you have seen him act. If he says "No," drop the subject and try again another time. If he agrees, then choose one behavior to work on. State the behavior you observed and the problem you think it is causing, in a matter-of-fact fashion. For example: "I see you frequently picking your nose. You may think no one notices, but actually they do. It might really be "grossing out" your friends."

Do not overwhelm your child with an entire list. Let him hear one behavior at a time and work on it for a couple of weeks. Also, do not get frustrated even if he does not appear to be listening to you, as he may just be embarrassed. Later on, he may mull over what you said.

CONCLUDING THOUGHTS:

Once your child has integrated some of your observations and has made efforts to correct them, he should be encouraged to work on developing friendships one step at a time. He should choose someone in the class who is at least partially sympathetic to him, and try to reach out to him first.

Of course, if your child is unable to integrate your criticisms and correct his behaviors, or manifests bizarre behaviors, you should seek competent professional help for your child. As with most problems, early intervention improves the prognosis greatly.

CHAPTER

23

❦

Avoiding Tantrums

*A*ll parents dread tantrums. There is nothing quite like the experience of being stuck on a long line at a supermarket, or on a crowded bus, and having your child wail and carry on. Though many people *know* that one should not give in to tantrums, some are unable to bear the excruciating kvetching, and often cave in to the child's demands. Obviously, if you give in to tantrums, it will encourage more tantrums; however, the purpose of this essay is not to belabor the obvious. In this chapter, we will discuss parenting methods that allow you to bypass and avoid situations that bring about tantrums, so you do not have to cause yourself and your child needless misery.

TANTRUMS AS CRISES OF CONTROL:

We have mentioned previously the concept of competency and control. Namely, that all humans, especially children, have a strong desire to master and control their environment. It is for this reason that the toddler-to-be bravely struggles to learn how to walk, despite repeated injuries and falls.

One can view a tantrum as a crisis of control. The child who is having a tantrum is desperately fighting for control over his life. For whatever reason, the child has fixated on a particular object, such as, a candy or a toy, and is fighting for dear life to possess it, as a drowning person lunges for a life preserver. It may seem silly or unnecessary to the parent, but for the moment, this object has taken on an epic significance in the life of the child. Hold this object back, and it's almost as if you are denying him his own life. That is why a tantrum is so emotionally powerful.

Having said this, it does not mean you should give in to tantrums. It is your job as a parent to teach your child about limits and reality. Just because Rachel feels that she is going to fall apart if she cannot have her lollipop, does not mean she will. However, if you understand the inner dynamic of the tantrum, you can learn how to prevent it from happening.

ADVANCE PREPARATION IS THE KEY:

If you think about it carefully, you will notice that most tantrums occur when a child is exposed to a rapid or unforeseen change in plans. When first retrospectively analyzing a situation that brought about a tantrum, it may not be obvious to you what the sudden change was, because you knew about it all along. However, if you persist in your inquiry, you will always discover this factor. For example, you are on the crowded bus and after fifteen minutes your child notices someone eating a candy. He then starts whining and carrying on for a candy. He is inconsolable and you are exasperated. Actually, what happened here is that your child was totally unprepared for the experience of a long and crowded bus ride. You knew all along that it would be a difficult trip home during rush hour, but he did not. You braced yourself psychologically for the stress, but he did not. On top of that, now he is hungry.

Have you ever been happily cruising along the highway at a time when you do not expect traffic, and then all of the sudden, get stuck in a totally unexpected standstill? First you hope it will clear up, but slowly the horror of it dawns on you as it goes on and on, mile after mile. How do you feel? Frustrated? Mad? Do you have an urge to cry out or pound the dashboard? Perhaps, but if this same traffic jam happened during your usual slow rush-hour commute, you would not be nearly as frustrated. The difference is, you are emotionally prepared for traffic during rush hour, but *not* early on a Sunday morning. The child on that bus was completely unprepared, and that is the cause of the tantrum. When a person is warned in advance, he is still able to maintain some sense of control by preparing himself emotionally for what is to come.

In order to give your child this sense of control, you might try saying something like this: "We are going on a trip. It will be a crowded, hot, and slow ride. You will need to drink and eat, but we won't be able to. Do you want to get a drink now? Do you want to choose a snack or a toy to play with?"

THE TOY STORE:

Even the notorious "I want this toy now!" tantrum has its roots in a lack of emotional preparation. Today, children are bombarded and overstimulated by all kinds of media that is insidiously and purposely designed to arouse in them a desire for the latest toy. Even children who do not watch television somehow know about and want the latest toy or action figure. The loud and seductive packaging, as well as the frenetic sights and sounds in aisle after aisle in a toy store, are too much for the barely formed personalities of children to resist without adequate coaching. (Woe unto the parents who expose their children to a steady diet of this junk from commercial television! But that is for another essay entirely.)

You can prepare your child before a trip to the toy store so he can have a chance to brace himself emotionally for what he will see and experience. You can say, "We are going to look for a present for your cousin David. In the store, you will see many different exciting-looking toys that you will wish you could have. It is the job of the toy store to make the toys look as exciting as possible. However, it is his birthday, not yours. We will not be getting a present for you. Do you want to come along, or stay at home? If you come along, we can keep a list of what you like. Then we can try to get one of those items next year for your birthday."

CONCLUDING THOUGHTS:

In the above examples, the key strategy is to give your child advance notice and some amount of choice, so you can allow him to feel some degree of control. He can choose what snack to bring on the bus, he can choose whether to come to the toy store, he can make a list of toys he would like, and so forth. This method can be applied in any area where you find your child susceptible to tantrums. Not only will it reduce the likelihood of tantrums, but it will also help your child develop an ability to exercise good judgment and planning skills.

24

꒒

Peer Pressure and
Family Values

$\mathcal{W}$e understand that our readers may have a wide range of religious standards and values. For example, some parents might have no problem with their children seeing the latest Disney movie, and others would have serious objections. Some might find particular dolls, trading cards, action toys, or fashion accessories to be objectionable, while others may think nothing of it. However, regardless of what your standards are as a parent, invariably, they will be tested as your children seek to fit into their peer groups.

This phenomenon is universal to all conscientious parents, regardless of their religion, beliefs, values, and culture. The sociological explanation for this is, though people generally associate with those who have similar values to them, in an entire group there is always one child who is from a family that has less stringent standards than your own. Of course, that one child's influence is all that is necessary to cause your children to wail, "All my friends have such and such. Why can't

I get it too?" Once again, it makes no difference whether the complaint is about a toy, a movie, earrings, a nose ring, or a tongue ring. The dilemma is the same. Do you uphold your personal standards and values and risk alienating your child from his or her friends and creating resentment, or do you cave in because "everyone else" is? Whatever your decision ultimately is, the outcome you are looking for is that your child comes to appreciate your values and does not rebel against them, because you are interested in winning the war, not the battle.

Feuerman's Peer-Pressure Postulate states, "Even if only one child has that particular toy or privilege, you will be told that *everyone* in the class has it." Not only is it important to clarify to what extent this claim is true, but it is also important to help your child match his perception with the reality so that he will feel more comfortable.

If it turns out that most of his peers do indeed have this item or this privilege, then it may be necessary to reevaluate your position. It is not fair to expect your child to be isolated and deprived. In most circumstances such as this, a parent can be flexible. However, sometimes it may not be possible. If you feel that the desired object or privilege is totally unacceptable, as a parent you have the right to take a stand for what you believe in. However, in that case, you should ask yourself why your child is in a school/neighborhood where the majority of his peers are involved in something that is against your values. You may need to consider changing schools, or even neighborhoods. Obviously, this is easier said than done, and if you truly are in such a situation, this thought has probably already crossed your mind. Nevertheless, it should be a serious consideration if this kind of conflict is constantly arising. If you are unsure how many peers truly have this privilege or toy, or are convinced that your child is exaggerating, the challenge is to find out the facts *and* to help change your child's perception that *everyone* has it. Below, we will describe an intervention that will allow you to learn more about your child's peer group and, at the same time, allow your child to learn more about your values.

A FACT-FINDING SURVEY:

For illustrative purposes, in this example, let us assume your 10-year-old daughter wants to wear those new platform sneakers. You think they are not particularly safe and also feel they are too provocative for a young girl to wear. Of course, your daughter tells you, "Everyone in my class is wearing them." Try telling her, "I am interested in learning more about these sneakers. I am also interested in why your friends like them so much and what they think about them. Before I make a decision about whether we will buy them, I want you to conduct a survey. Go around, and interview your classmates. Make a list of each of your friends in your class that has these sneakers, and next to their name, write down why they like having them. Come back to me with your survey and let's discuss your results." This exercise can even be conducted by a very young grade-schooler. The rule of thumb is, if she is smart and savvy enough to want what her friends want, she ought to be smart enough to talk to them and gather information.

This exercise works wonders because it operates on many levels:

1. It gives your child a sense of control, since she is no longer helpless in the decision-making process. At the same time, it keeps you in firm control as the parent and decision maker.
2. It gives you much-needed information regarding what her peers' values are, and how many, in fact, do follow this fad.
3. It helps your child see her desire to be a part of the crowd in a more objective light, by engaging her rational faculties. In addition, she will be exposed to a vari-

ety of views as she interviews her friends. She may even hear about how some are already bored of the sneakers or feel they are too cumbersome.

Your child may balk and complain that this exercise is unfair and beside the point, but you should hold firm. In order for this to work though, it can't be just "busy work." You have to show genuine interest and openness to what this survey might discover, and be willing to consider allowing her to wear these sneakers if the facts warrant. If you are sincere, your child will sense this and cooperate.

CONCLUDING THOUGHTS:

When peer pressures conflict with parental values, parents are often in a position of either compromising or lowering their standards, or feeling that they are depriving their children of something "all their friends have." Neither choice is optimal. In this article, we described an effective and emotionally sound approach that engages your child and avoids provoking resentment, by including your child in a real examination of her and her peers' values.

25

ॐ

How to Praise Children

$\mathcal{M}$ost parents would be surprised to discover what children really understand when we talk to them. Language is heavily dependent upon cultural context and mutual shared experience. The younger children are, the less of a context they have to draw upon when it comes to interpreting what is said to them. For the most part, children give the impression of listening and comprehension when in fact they assume you are pleased or displeased merely from the tone of your voice. As an experiment, after praising your child for something he did, ask him what you just said. You may find out that he either understood only part of it, or may have completely misunderstood what you said.

Parents of teenagers, don't think this article does not apply to you. True, your teenager ought to be able to fully *comprehend* what you are saying, but that's assuming he or she is listening! To get to that point, however, may require some technique.

In this article, we will discuss some of the common pitfalls in the process of praising your child, as well as provide some interventions to maximize communication and enhance your child's internalization of your remarks.

THE USE AND MISUSE OF PRAISE:

The goal of parental praise is to encourage behavior that you deem to be positive. For example, let us say Shira did her homework right away, without anyone telling her to. At that point, Mom will want to encourage Shira to repeat this behavior, so she will try to communicate that she is very pleased about what she did.

However, sometimes parents give false praise either as wishful thinking or in a vain effort to enhance their child's self-esteem. Returning to the example above, suppose Shira only sat down with her notebook, and then started chewing her pen and daydreamed? If Shira has a history of delaying her homework, Mom might have an urge to start praising Shira right away, hoping that this will encourage her to continue. Or, suppose Shira's performance as a student is generally poor. When Mom looks at her barely legible homework, even though only two answers are correct, she may have the urge to say, "Great job!" In both of these cases, the praise is going to be useless in encouraging Shira to improve her behavior and habits. This is because almost every child is quite well aware of the quality of his or her work. If you praise her for something she has done and she feels she does not deserve it, you are causing her to feel guilty for something she did not earn. On the other hand, in both of the examples above, Shira *did* do something praiseworthy, and the trick is to be honest about it, so the praise is genuine. We will return to these examples shortly to illustrate how best to do this, but first we need to take a detour into Shira's deeper thoughts. (For the purpose of brevity, henceforth, the two cases above will be referred to as "Lazy Shira" and "Poor-Student Shira.")

PRAISE THE BEHAVIOR, NOT THE CHILD:

Even regarding our original example of Shira who did a superb job with her homework, if you praise her by telling her she is a "super student" or a "good girl," you risk diminishing the effectiveness of the praise. This is because people are quite complex, and though Shira may indeed have done a good thing, she may not necessarily feel that she is a "good girl" for a variety of reasons. Perhaps, she resents her homework or she resents you and does not *feel* like doing the homework but does it anyway. You may be pleased that she complied, but she may feel guilty for harboring thoughts of rebellion. Or, perhaps the homework was really easy tonight and did not require as much effort as you thought it did. So Shira thinks, "I am not such a good girl. If the homework was hard, I would have avoided it as usual." It would be far more accurate to praise Shira's behavior. You can tell her, "I see you did your homework. It makes me happy to see you do your homework right away."

Returning to our previous examples of the "Lazy Shira" and "Poor-Student Shira," the goal is to identify the actions and behaviors that are positive without praising her for something she *knows* she did not do. You can tell "Lazy Shira," "I see you sat down right away. It makes me happy to see you get ready to work so quickly. Now, how about doing the homework and making me even happier?" You can say to "Poor-Student Shira," "I see two correct answers on the page. I am glad that you got two answers right. Now if you check and correct some more of them, I will be very pleased."

In addition, after stating your own feelings of pleasure regarding this behavior, you should ask your child how he or she feels about it. Aside from verifying that she actually heard and understood what you said, you are also giving your child a chance to review and internalize your remarks. This will increase the likelihood that this behavior will be repeated and extended.

CONCLUDING THOUGHTS:

Many parents make the mistake of overpraising or falsely prais-ing their children. Even when praise is well deserved, your child may not always feel that he deserves it, due to his own per-sonal experiences and thoughts. When praising children, it is best to:

1. State the facts briefly and clearly. Try to keep it to one or two sentences.
2. Do not exaggerate or in any way inflate your comments.
3. State how you feel about what he or she did.
4. Ask your child how he feels about what he did, to see if he understands what you are saying and agrees.

If you follow these techniques, you will increase the effec-tiveness of your praise and gradually, but significantly, encour-age positive behaviors.

CHAPTER

26

❧

Blowing Up At Your Kids

*D*id you ever have a morning where, as a parent, every minor disobedience seems to pile up until you find yourself in a screaming rage? For example, after you finally blow up at Shloime for leaving his clothes on the bathroom floor, your other children kind of slink around the house, trying to stay out of your way, hoping they are not next on your list. After a couple of minutes, you may feel ashamed and guilty of your outburst, and worried about the effect that it has had on your child. Since you are already in an irritable mood, these thoughts only contribute to your misery, leaving you vulnerable to blowing up a second or third time over the next annoyance. Like aftershocks from an earthquake, no one is completely sure when the ordeal will finally end.

"AT LEAST I REALLY TAUGHT HIM A LESSON!"

You may try to console yourself with the fact that at least you really "taught him a lesson" and he will never do it again. Unfortunately, experience shows that this is usually not the case. Parental blowups are no different from tantrums. In fact, you did teach your child a couple of lessons, just not the ones you think. You taught your child:

1. Shouting and screaming, instead of talking calmly, solves problems.
2. Parents can be crazy and out of control.
3. Parents should be obeyed not because they are older, and wiser—just because they are bigger and stronger.

At this point you might be thinking, "True, but surely he at least now knows how upset I am and will be more careful to obey me in the future." Not so fast. Think about it, when your child has a tantrum, is he actually intelligible or understandable? Much of the time, you cannot even figure out exactly what the problem is, let alone work to solve it. Well, you might think that it should be perfectly clear what you are upset about, but your child may be so overloaded and shell-shocked by your fierce anger, that he may tune out everything you say.

After you have had a blowup, just as an experiment, ask your child if he understands what you are upset about. Don't take yes for an answer. Ask him to explain it in his own words. You may be surprised to understand how little he actually absorbed. He might say, "You got angry 'cause I left a sock on the floor." Your child is bound to be confused and unable to take this matter very seriously, because how many times have socks been left on the floor and no one got mad? This is hardly a capital offense. At best, your child will think, "OK, Mom is in a bad mood, so I'll be a little more considerate for a few hours." Of course, you really are upset about his attitude of noncaring, and his not being neat. Perhaps, in general, he is negligent in his chores. Whatever the case may be, he will not understand this from your explosive outburst.

DAMAGE CONTROL:

Once you have had an outburst, if you are the "feel guilty" type, you may want to apologize to your child. Although your intentions are honorable, this is not the best course of action. Asking your child to forgive you for an outburst is like your boss asking you for forgiveness after he screams at you. He's your boss, so you'll say "Yes," but secretly, you resent him even more. What you really want from him is to make your work environment professional and pleasant, you actually couldn't care less about forgiveness. So too, with your child. He will feel pressure to forgive you in order to make *you* feel better, but it is useless in making him feel better.

The best approach is to wait until you are calm, and then ask him if he understands why you were upset. Continue discussing it until you feel that the matter is clear. Then, you should acknowledge his feelings and experience. You can say, "Was it scary for you when I screamed at you? How did it feel for you?" After listening carefully to his response, you can then sympathize with him. If you are comfortable apologizing, you can do so now, but don't make a big deal of it. You should mention that you know it is better to discuss things calmly, and you will try to do so the next time he makes you angry.

PREVENTATIVE MEDICINE:

Though this is easier said than done, if you are blowing up at your children, you need to learn how to monitor your frustration level. When you find yourself reaching the limit, you should think about what the core issue is, instead of waiting until you get into a rage over a minor detail. If you can discuss this with your spouse and get the benefit of a second opinion and insight, it would be even better.

The fact is, it takes a long time to shape a child's behavior. For example, If you want to succeed at improving your child's

cooperation around the house, you will need to be patient.
You should find the time to explain what you are upset about
and try to make it have meaning for him. If he is constantly
leaving dirty clothes around and not putting away his school
stuff, you should tell him: "When your things are left around
the house, it makes me feel like my home is a mess and ugly.
This is like if I kept all of my pots and pans in your bedroom.
After a while, you would feel very unhappy about your personal space being so cluttered. For adults, the living room is
our personal space, and we need it kept neat."

With younger children, you may also need to link desired behavior to some kind of incentive. A chart with stars works well.
Be sure that the reward is modest and agreed upon in advance.
If the prize is too big, your child will learn how to manipulate
you into buying bigger and bigger prizes. Also, try to depict it
graphically so your child can visually watch his stars add up in
a column, until they reach the picture of the prize. (Interestingly, Maimonides mentions motivational prizes as a method
for teaching children proper behavior. See his introduction to
his commentary on Mishna *Sanhedrin Perek Chelek*.)

As a final word, be as patient and forgiving with yourself, as
you would like to be with your child. It takes time to learn how
to avoid and manage the inevitable frustrations of parenting.
Your children do not need perfection, just an environment where
they can learn how to succeed in the world.

27

&

The Teeter-Totter Syndrome

$\mathcal{S}$ome families suffer from a peculiar form of sibling rivalry, namely, that each sibling behaves as if there is a central pot of gifts, talents, and skills in the family. The tyranny of this rivalry is that no two siblings can excel in the same area, because there is only one of each kind of skill available. For example, one child may be the studious bookish kind, and the other a "sports jock." One daughter may act very feminine and the other more "tomboyish." Even when both siblings have academic interests, one may carve out math to be his specialty and claim that "reading is boring," while another sibling favors literature, and claims, "I just can't do math." Some family therapists call this the Teeter-Totter Effect, because the siblings act as if they are on a seesaw. Just as on a seesaw, for one person to rise the other *must* descend; so too, only one child can be "up" in one skill area at a time.

In this chapter, we will discuss how to correctly diagnose the Teeter-Totter Effect, a psychological theory of its origin, and some parenting interventions to help free children from its grip.

DIAGNOSING THE TEETER-TOTTER SYNDROME:

Of course, there is such a thing as natural talent and personal disposition. Each sibling may indeed gravitate to areas where they feel most competent based on their own unique abilities. That is perfectly normal behavior. However, sometimes parents or teachers get a distinct feeling that their child is just shutting down and avoiding an area where he or she may have enormous potential. Though there is no way to be sure that your family is suffering from the Teeter-Totter Syndrome, there are some telltale signs, which we have listed below:

1. In general, there is a great deal of rivalry and competition among siblings in the family.
2. When one child in the family improves in one area, another child "fills in the slack" by regressing in another area. For example, Joshua's behavior has improved dramatically. He has become responsible with his homework and now helps out a lot around the house. Oddly, Elana who used to be "mommy's little helper" has begun to be irritable and moody.
3. A child who generally has good intelligence, aptitude, and study habits, steadfastly avoids even trying to work on a certain skill. He or she just says, "I'm no good at this."
4. Each of your children seems to have a unique role and specialty in the family. Pay careful attention to same-sex siblings who are close in age. It is among that subgroup that the greatest polarity occurs. Some examples of roles and specialties:
   a. *talmid chochom*/rebbetzin
   b. sports jock/athlete
   c. wiseguy/joker
   d. whimsical, "spacey" artist
   e. baby

f. serious businessman
g. professional
h. technology/computer "nerd"
i. healer

The above signs should be thought of as merely ideas to get you thinking. When it comes to subtle matters such as this, it is your gut instinct and intuition as parents that carry the most weight.

A PSYCHOLOGICAL THEORY:

What is the cause of the Teeter-Totter Syndrome? Why do many siblings seem to behave as if there is only one highly rationed source in the family for talents and skills that only one child can use at a time? Although this teeter-totter dynamic can occur in any place of birth order and in any size family, for simplicity's sake, let us examine the hypothetical case of Debby and Elana.

Debby is a bookworm. She comes to school with sloppy, unbrushed hair. Most of the time Debby has her head stuck in a book. On the other hand, her younger sister, Elana, is very feminine and sweet. She is popular with her friends and has excellent taste in clothes. Though Elana is not a poor student, her teachers report that she underperforms. Elana would rather spend her Sundays working on a play with her friends than a book report. Debby is an excellent student but is socially withdrawn. In such a case, one gets the overwhelming impression that Elana and Debby are each half of a person. Wouldn't it be ideal if Elana could borrow some of Debby's academic diligence, and Debby could borrow some of Elana's social acumen?

Let us go back in time and try to reconstruct what factors could have helped each of these siblings select different paths: Debby was once the only child. After Elana was born, everyone "*kvelled*" about Elana's cute blond curls. Though Debby was far from ugly, this was not an area that she felt she could compete in. First, Elana was younger and automatically more cute. Second, Elana has the most amazingly golden hair. However, the one clear advantage Debby discovered, was that she had a two-year head start on life. Debby realized that she could get attention from her parents by displaying her intellectual and cognitive achievements. Looking at this matter from Elana's perspective, and as potentially intelligent as she may be, what could she gain by trying to compete with Debby? She started out with an immediate two-year handicap. At best, she could hope for a stalemate. However, through her own natural attractiveness and ample reinforcement by her family, Elana chose to get her attention through her socialization skills.

As we have mentioned previously, according to some psychological theories, there is a basic human drive to be competent. This drive is what pushes a toddler to bravely struggle to learn how to walk, despite the pain of many falls. Here too, Elana and Debby chose their respective paths in an effort to be competent. The one clear advantage Debby discovered is that she had a two-year head start on life. Debby realized that she could get attention from her parents by displaying her intellectual and cognitive achievements.

(Please note that we use the word "choose" in a psychological sense. A psychological choice does not mean that the person sat and thought about it. However, it does mean that a developmental path was taken by the organism in response to its environment. What a person "chooses" unconsciously may not be what they want *consciously*.) Thus, according to this psychological explanation, the Teeter-Totter Syndrome results from a specialized form of sibling rivalry. It then follows to reason that if parents can reduce the rivalry in the family system, their children will be less influenced by their sibling's choices, and make decisions that are more genuinely representative of their true inclinations and talents.

HOW TO FREE YOUR FAMILY FROM THE TEETER-TOTTER SYNDROME:

Unfortunately such a dynamic is common among siblings, and to some extent a hazard of family living. Nevertheless, some interventions and strategies can be employed to reduce its intensity. These interventions are subtle, so the changes will most likely not be dramatic. However, slowly and over time, they can have a positive impact.

1. As a parent, make it a habit to praise actions instead of children. For example, *don't* say, "Boy you got a 100 on your test; you are a real math whiz!" Instead, *do* say, "A 100 on a math test is a great thing. It must feel good to get such a good grade." Or instead of, "You are a great athlete," you can say, "It must feel good to be good at sports." This allows you to freely praise your children without fear of creating jealousy, because you are not favoring any child over the other by adding additional credit or praise, rather you are joining the child in reinforcing the feelings of pride he or she already has. In addition, this prevents reinforcing the idea that one person owns a particular trait, since you are reflecting upon how it must feel good to do well in a particular subject, and not labeling anyone as "owning it." The subtle message here is, "Anyone can do this. Whoever chooses to do so, can enjoy this feeling of accomplishment."

2. Discuss and give greater exposure to various adult models and archetypes that are outside of the immediate sibling family, but still inside the family constellation. For example, Uncle Nate may be the businessman in the family, *Zeide* Nosson is the *talmid chochom*, *Tanta* Malka is the successful career and mother type, and *Tanta* Esty is a successful teacher. This can help in two ways:

a. As your children learn more about other family members, they will have other models to draw from, thereby diminishing the intensity of their rivalry.

b. In addition, once they are exposed to different lifestyle choices than their immediate siblings, they may be able to look at their own position in the family more objectively.

3. Lastly, interpret the teeter-totter dynamic to your children in a language that they can grasp. You might say something like, "I notice that in this family no two people allows themselves to be good in a particular area at the same time. Does anyone else notice this?" Sometimes, when people are made aware that they are under the influence of an inner (and possibly unconscious) rule, they become freer to reevaluate and change their behavior. When you talk about this with your children, do not get overinvolved, or say it over and over again. Just mention it calmly and neutrally as an observation. This will decrease the likelihood of any unconscious defenses being activated to prevent confronting a potentially disturbing revelation. Even if your children do not show much of a reaction, be patient. You may have planted a seed that will take time to grow.

28

꒰ꜙ

Children, *Shul*,
and Davening

𝒟oes this scene seem familiar to you?

Dovid: "Daddy, how many minutes until *shul* is over?"
Dad: "Ummmmm, shhhhh."
Dovid: "I'm thirsty!"
Dad: "Uhhhh, uhh, mmmm, shhh."
Dovid: "TAP, TAP, TAP, TAP, TAP, FIDGET, SQUIRM,
   TAP."
Dad: "Dovid! Shhhh!"

Many parents experience acute distress and embarrassment over their children's behavior in *shul*. For many, managing children in *shul* seems to be a never-ending struggle, where both parents and children often end up feeling resentful, worn-out, and negative about davening. In this essay, we will address in detail the sociological, psychological, and religious dynamics of the *shul* experience from a pedagogical perspective. We also will provide practical suggestions for behavior modification and management to enhance your and your child's davening.

Successful management of children during davening requires an approach that utilizes a variety of parenting techniques, in addition to demanding from children an unusual amount of self-discipline and delay of gratification. The single most important factor in all good parenting is planning ahead. Parents must be proactive in anticipating what the environment will be like and preparing the child in advance by informing him of his behavioral-performance expectations and responsibilities, as well as having an appropriate reward and punishment system in place.

Creating and implementing a plan for improving your child's behavior during davening requires that you assess many factors that contribute to his ability to behave properly in *shul*. Areas to address are:

1. For this child's age and developmental level, in other situations outside of *shul*, what duration of time can the child be expected to sit still?
2. For this child in particular, what duration of sitting still in *shul* is his normal baseline behavior?
3. What parts of *tefila* does the child know and should be expected to participate in?
4. When a child misbehaves in *shul*, what feasible disciplinary action can taken by the parent that least disrupts the parent's and other congregants' *davening*?
5. Is there an area where the child can play safely, if the parent allows for a break?
6. What is the general environment of the *shul*?
   a. Is the *shul* crowded?
   b. Is the temperature and climate comfortable or hot and stuffy?
   c. Do the adults maintain proper decorum (e.g. no excessive talking during *davening*)?
   d. Is the *nusach hatefila* interesting and enjoyable (e.g., do they sing during *davening*)? Is there an unusual amount of interruptions such as *misheberachs* and *hosafos*?

e. Is there a rabbi's speech? If so, how long?

In addition, children require consistency. Therefore it is imperative that you formulate, clarify, and articulate, for yourself and your spouse, your family's values regarding davening, and then set the behavioral objectives to be compatible with these values. Some examples of value matters to consider are:

1. At what age is it acceptable to play outside of *shul*?
2. At what age is the child expected to answer to *kaddish, kedusha*, say the entire *davening*, and so forth.?
3. At what age is eating allowed inside *shul*? Outside shul before *kiddush*?
4. What is your family's practice regarding talking in *shul*? Never? Only if urgent? Between *aliyos*? Always?

Obviously, if the adults are not clear on these issues, then the children also will be unclear and confused.

DEFINING THE BEHAVIORAL GOALS:

Whenever you are trying to improve your child's behavior, it is critical that you set goals that are realistic and appropriate for his particular age and developmental level. Davening in shul requires many different and discrete skills; therefore it can be easy to become frustrated with your child's failure to "behave," even though he may in fact be performing well in some areas. Examples of the skills required for *davening* in *shul* include:

1. The ability to sit still without fidgeting, tapping, or disturbing other *mispallelim* (congregants).
2. The ability to follow and read from a *siddur*.
3. The ability to delay gratification and hold off from talking or whining at improper times.

4. The ability to self-manage minor hygiene issues without disturbing the parent's *davening*, (e.g., going to the bathroom, obtaining tissues and blowing his nose, getting a drink from the water fountain, etc).

It is necessary to establish a baseline of your child's behavior in each of these areas, and then set about helping him to improve them as individual problems. Every few weeks, it may only be possible to work on one of these areas. However, if you focus on one area at a time, and implement appropriate punishments and rewards (which we will discuss later in this chapter), the chance of success is much greater. This is because, not only will it be easier for you and your child to concentrate on one area at a time, it will also allow your child to develop pride and confidence as he achieves the goals. In addition, this will prevent you and him from being frustrated with future failures, because instead of saying "Your behavior during davening was 'bad,'" you can specifically praise areas of success and point out the areas of shortcoming in a more rational and supportive manner. Remember the Talmudic adage, "If you try to grab too much, you will not be able to hold on to it. If you grab onto a small portion, then you will be able to hold on to it." (*Rosh Hashanah*, 4b.)

PLANNING IN ADVANCE:

As we have mentioned, successful parenting requires planning in advance and preparation. It will be easier for your child to behave if he is spending some of his time in *shul* actually participating in *davening* instead of being bored. For younger children, you should ask your child's rebbe or teacher what amount and what parts of *davening* your child recites every day in school. You should then prepare your child in advance by showing him and perhaps marking off with paper clips what he is expected to say. You may want to add on one or two things for *Shabbos davening*, such as the key part of *Shacharis Shemoneh Esrei*, and *Musaf*, and have your child rehearse his reading with you. Space out his davening so he does not rush through it in five minutes. Instead, develop a hand-signal system, so he can read parts of *davening* that are synchronized with the rest of the *shul*. It is preferable to use a siddur identical or similar to his school siddur. For older children, in a firm and serious tone, communicate as specifically and as clearly as possible which kinds of behavior are acceptable and which are not, and what rewards or actions you will take should they comply or fail. The older the child is, the more autonomous and independent he should be. You may consider allowing him to take breaks or stretches as appropriate. That alone may be a sufficient reward, for example, "If you follow the behavior and performance guidelines I set, then you can freely take five- to ten-minute breaks whenever you need to."

However, aside from the behavioral interventions, you also want to help your children find meaning, purpose, and emotional value in davening. A trained seal can be taught to jump through hoops using behavior modification, and so can a child be trained to behave, but we also want our children enjoy the davening as well. Aside from the behavioral interventions, we want to help our children find meaning, purpose, and emotional value in davening.

DAVENING FROM A CHILD'S PERSPECTIVE:

What is *shul* like from your child's emotional perspective? In truth, *davening* is really an activity that only a mature adult can appreciate fully. Normal healthy children do not feel excessively anxious or worried about the future, nor are they plagued with existential dilemmas about the meaning of life. They are likely to feel the least need to pray for health, financial success, and spiritual guidance. In addition, children have a limited ability to translate the *davening*, and beyond the literal translation, an even more limited ability to extract the poetic, metaphoric, and emotional content of the prayers. On the other hand, our tradition is that it is a mitzvah to introduce our children to *davening* at a relatively early age (see Maimonides *Yad, Laws of Torah Study*, 1:6), so we can infer from this that children can find meaning and purpose in their *davening*. Therefore, concomitant to any behavioral-modification programs you set into place, you should engage your child in an ongoing discussion and exploration of the meaning of prayer. In this exploration, you should try to have your child talk as much as possible without lecturing at him. With patience and self-control on your part, this can be achieved by maintaining a genuinely curious and open-minded approach toward learning about your child's thoughts in this area. You should help you child explore important questions such as:

1. Does he feel that he can talk to God and He will listen?
2. Are there any things that he wants to pray for?
3. Can he understand how the mitzvah of loving God is expressed in *davening*?
4. Can he understand how the mitzvah of fearing God is expressed in *davening*?
5. What is the meaning of the Shema?
6. What is the meaning of *Shemone Esrei*?
7. Can he find any value in sitting quietly in shul, even when he is "finished with his davening?" (Even some children can be taught to develop an appreciation for quiet contemplation. In fact, a normal developmental behavior for children is to spend a large portion of awake time daydreaming. When your child isn't busy davening, it may be a good strategy for him to "daydream" in *shul*. The melodies and chants of the adults are still being absorbed with a hopefully beneficial spiritual effect.)

Of course, another serious emotional matter to consider is your own honest feelings about *davening*. If davening is interesting and meaningful to you, then your children will automatically get this message over time and incorporate it into their own personalities. However, if you feel that davening is a duty and a chore, chafe or glance irritably at your watch during an extended *davening* or long-winded rabbi's speech, you can hardly expect your child to feel otherwise. In addition, children are more limited in their ability to conceal and control their feelings, so if you are just mildly irritated and restless, you can expect your child to be bouncing and fidgeting in a less-than-subtle fashion. If you really do feel that your *shul's davening* is "too long," in order to model proper behavior for your child, it is necessary either to increase your capacity to tolerate and appreciate the *davening*, or switch to a shul that is more compatible with your particular needs. Remember, children do not learn how to behave from what you tell them. Rather, they learn how to behave by watching what you do and picking up on how you feel!

Below are some useful interventions to help improve your child's behavior in *shul*:

TELLING TIME:

It would be helpful for your younger child to know how to tell time, analog or digital, and have the ability to find out the time on his own. He can then be told in advance when davening approximately ends, or for how long he is expected to stay, and then not need to ask you every two minutes, "What time is it?"

TALKING TO YOUR CHILD DURING *DAVENING*:

If you do not want to get irritated and frustrated, you should decide when, where, how, and if you will talk to your child in *shul*. (It may also be helpful to get halachic clarity from a rabbi as to when or if it is permitted to talk to your child during *davening* in order to instruct him.) Whatever parameters you set for talking, make sure your child understands them in advance, and stick to them consistently. It also is helpful to develop and rehearse with your child a few agreed-upon hand signals for words such as, "yes," "no," "sit," "stand," "I am warning you . . .", "Do not bother me now. I am concentrating," "quiet," "Go to Mommy," "I am proud of you—you are doing great," and so forth.

IF YOU NEED TO DISCIPLINE YOUR CHILD IN *SHUL*:

Sometimes you will need to discipline your child in *shul*. Plan in advance what kinds of disciplinary actions can realistically be done during *davening*. If you have been able to set up a system where your child can take breaks, perhaps you want to increase the duration and number based on behavior. If so, make it all clear in advance, so your child has something to work toward.

If your child is really out of control, you should have a system in place where if need be, you take him and have him removed from *shul* as quickly as possible. Mother and Father should discuss in advance how and who will do this. There is no point in engaging in a power struggle for the rest of *davening*. After *davening*, you can follow up with appropriate discipline. If it is a chronic problem, you may need to consider setting more simple behavioral objectives until he can master them, such as limiting the amount of time he is expected to stay in *shul* altogether. Over time you can increase your expectations as he continues to succeed.

RUNNING AROUND:

Some parents let their children run around freely in or outside of *shul*, while others do not. If you feel it is OK to let your child run around during an agreed-upon "break time," make sure the children are playing in a safe place and are engaging in relatively safe activities. Consider working with other parents to set up a rotation system of adults who supervise.

Personally, we are not in favor of letting children run wild, even outside of *shul*. First, it is not in the quiet contemplative spirit of *davening*. Second, it is seldom safe enough. However, you can let your child have stretching breaks, and walking around and talking breaks. Review with your child what kinds of behavior are acceptable and what is not. Even if other children run around, you child can be taught to follow your expectations. An important incentive might be whether you will allow him to take breaks on his own and monitor by himself for how long.

CONCLUDING THOUGHTS:

Many parents experience acute distress and embarrassment over their children's behavior in *shul*. For many, managing children in *shul* seems to be a never ending struggle, where both parents and children often end up feeling resentful, worn-out, and negative about *davening*. However, the proactive, organized, and thoughtful approach that we have detailed in this essay, if utilized on a consistent basis, will help almost any child improve over time.

❧

When a *Yeshiva Bochur* and His Family Disagree Over *Frumkeit*

*A*s psychotherapists, we have encountered families in treatment where disagreements over some aspect or ideology of learning in Israel figured prominently. Furthermore, in many instances, as we began to explore other stated problems, this issue emerged as an area of significant tension and familial conflict.

Some examples of the conflicts are:

1. The son or daughter wants to spend a year learning in yeshiva/seminary, but the family cannot afford it.
2. There is a disagreement about which yeshiva/seminary is appropriate.
3. The son or daughter wants to spend "just one more year" studying, while the parents feel that he or she needs to return home to begin college or a career.
4. The son or daughter does not want to come home at all, and wants to "make aliyah."

What makes these disagreements so difficult for families is that they revolve around deeply held religious principles on the one hand, and equally significant fears and practical concerns for the future on the other. In addition, matters become even more complicated in cases where the child's rebbe or teacher is encouraging and supporting a choice that the parents are not in favor of.

In this chapter, we will explore this complex issue from a sociological, religious, and psychological perspective, and offer interventions and strategies to improve communication and understanding among family members. Your child's year spent learning in Israel may be one of the most significant emotional, spiritual, and psychological experiences in his life. It will certainly have an impact. Let us begin to look at some of these issues in depth.

A STRUGGLE OVER RELIGIOUS VALUES:

Since this stage corresponds with the tail end of adolescence, it often is a catalyst for many far-reaching life decisions. Often these decisions upset the balance of the family, as they involve seemingly abrupt departures from parental expectations. Interestingly, we have observed this phenomenon in many families, and it seems to occur independently of how religious or "modern" a family is. The specific points of contention may differ from a more religious to a more secular family, but the basic pattern is the same. This pattern involves the adolescent questioning and challenging the values and beliefs of his or her family of origin, and as part of forming an identity for him or herself, the adolescent may choose to follow religious practices and stringencies that set him or her apart from the family. In one highly observant and rabbinical family we know of (quoted with their permission) this stage of life was labeled as The Kellogg's Isn't Kosher Phase. This nomenclature originated from the sons coming home from *mesivta*, and declaring the foods in the house to be of questionable *kashrus.* (Readers please note: We have no expert knowledge regarding *kashrus* of any Kellogg's product—this family's story took place in the 1970s. Today's yeshiva *bochurim* are more likely to challenge their families' *kashrus* standards regarding *yoshon*, insects in vegetables, nontithed imported fruits from Israel, and *cholov yisrael.*)

Therefore, a religious transformation of some sort is almost inevitable for these young and impressionable men and women who spend a year of study away from home. The experience in Israel is overwhelming, as they are confronted with many symbols of their roots and traditions. Furthermore, this may be the first time in their lives that they have experienced the ability to act in public as a fully religious Jew, with little fear or embarrassment.

After some initial surprise and discomfort, emotionally healthy and religiously sincere families will tolerate and even support these religious changes, regardless of whether it is in agreement with the family's current beliefs and practices. It only becomes problematic when on the basis of newly assimilated religious priorities or philosophies, the child begins to make decisions that have long-term and possibly harmful implications for the future. In some cases, a child may want to stay in yeshiva to study for an additional year, or he may reject the idea of pursuing a career other than Torah study. This may cause some parents to be concerned that their child may "wake up" many years later and find himself in financially oppressive circumstances. In addition to concern about their child's future, parents may feel anxious about being burdened with supporting an adult child or their grandchildren at a time in life when they looked forward to reducing their financial burdens and retiring. In response, parents may spend long hours arguing, trying to convince their child that they are "right." The child in turn may invoke the religious principles of his or her rabbis and teachers whom he or she has come to admire, as proof that he/she should have *bitachon* (faith) and place learning Torah above all mundane pursuits. All in all, this can be a painful and emotionally trying experience for both parties.

Aside from parents' own fears about their child becoming a financial burden, they also may wonder, "Is this choice an escape and excuse to avoid responsibility of the 'real world?'" In particular, if the child has shown in the past to have a personality pattern where he or she avoids responsibility, parents may be even more worried about the child's future.

We are aware that there are different and conflicting *hashkafos* regarding this matter, and in this column we are in no way attempting to take sides. What we can offer parents who have such concerns, are guidelines and suggestions that will help to minimize conflict and maximize understanding.

GUIDELINES:

Avoid arguing about religious values. You cannot forcibly convince a child of that age that *you* are right and he is wrong. This is one you cannot win. As we stated in prior articles, your child is following the teachings of his or her rabbis and mentors, and you cannot expect otherwise. Both parties should agree to enter into a discussion with an open mind to the other's opinion. As a parent, it may be difficult for you to "switch gears" from expecting and demanding compliance to engaging in a discussion. However, your child is almost an adult, and the best you can do is to offer your personal opinion and beliefs in a calm but firm manner, without getting all riled up. Even if it does not appear that way, over the long run, your child will be likely to consider what you have to say.

WHEN PARENTS FEEL THE YESHIVA IS WORKING AGAINST THEM:

In some cases, parents may encounter their child's rebbe or *rosh yeshiva* encouraging him or her to continue a course of study or maintain a religious philosophy that is contrary to parental wishes. This can be very frustrating for parents and painful for the yeshiva student. Before we make any concrete suggestions as to how to cope with this situation, it is important to understand the dynamics of this problem from both its halachic and sociological origins.

Halachically, there is much precedent and support for the idea that a child is not required to obey his parents when it comes to matters of preference in Torah study. (See *Shulchan Aruch, Yoreh Deah*, 240:13.) According to the Midrash, although Yaakov *Avinu* was punished for the time he spent away from home working for Lavan, he was *not* held liable for the time he spent studying Torah at *Yeshivas Shem V'ever*. (See Talmud *Megila* 16b.)

Sociologically, the American yeshiva movement in its early years was *built* on the basis of its young students rejecting the values of their parents and choosing a life more connected with Torah. In those days, it must have taken great courage to shun the American way of life and stand out "like a sore thumb" by returning to an "antiquated" religious practice. In order to accomplish this uphill and upstream battle, presumably the *roshei yeshiva* had to fortify and train their students to disregard popular sentiment and family mores in exchange for their noble calling. Though times have changed, and the standards and practices have become considerably more observant, this emotional undercurrent remains in yeshivas today. The explicit goal of a yeshiva is to teach Torah; however, the implicit goal is to elevate standards of observance in order to help preserve the yeshiva way of life in the face of pressures to conform to values alien to the Torah. In other words, if a child is sent to a yeshiva or seminary, *there is an expectation that he or she will be made more religious than his or her parents in order to fortify his or her observance.* And, even if the parents are quite religious, there are always new standards and levels to achieve. If we are correct in identifying this to be an implicit part of the yeshiva approach, parents can hardly expect the yeshiva's administration to defer to or consult with them regarding their child's religious training and values. (Please note, we are neither criticizing nor endorsing this feature of the yeshiva educational system. Rather, we are observing and interpreting this phenomenon in order to give people the tools to respond out of knowledge and sensitivity toward the underlying issues.)

"INDEPENDENCE" AND PERSONAL AUTONOMY:

As we have mentioned, the year of study in Israel may be the longest period of time that your child ever spent away from home, and allowed the most "independence" and personal autonomy that he ever experienced. We put quotation marks around the word "independence" because, in fact, it is an *illusion* of independence funded courtesy of Mom and Dad. However, it is precisely the illusory nature of it that is significant. Your child gets a chance to *feel* like an adult with very few actual adult responsibilities. In addition, many yeshivas have relatively broad curriculums and often there are few concrete academic demands (e.g., most do not grade or test their students). This observation is more applicable to yeshivos than to seminaries. Keeping that in mind, it is easy to understand how it might be difficult for a child to return to a world of chores and responsibilities, or to begin the process of secular academic instruction after having spent so much time without being bound to these demands.

Please note: We are not writing this as a criticism of the yeshiva *derech*. It is well known that most yeshiva students acquire valuable religious instruction and life skills during this year or two of study. The many yeshivas that do not place emphasis on concrete grade and study performance are following a traditional style of learning that some would argue is a part of the *mesorah* (oral tradition). Our goal is not to pass judgment on this approach; rather, we are attempting to objectively describe one possible psychological impact of this experience.

INTERVENTIONS TO HELP FOSTER TRUE INDEPENDENCE:

Some parents may fear that their child is hiding consciously or unconsciously behind this religious stance to avoid taking responsibility for his future. In a case where a child has a history of avoiding responsibility, these fears may be well founded. These parents complain, "Now, all of the sudden, Mr. or Ms. Irresponsible is ready to shoulder the financial struggle of *kollel* life for the sake of high religious values?"

What can you do as a parent to help your child develop a balanced and realistic outlook? To help your son or daughter develop more of a sense of "real-world" financial responsibilities, consider having your child present you with a budget for the year of study. After all, the dictum of *pas bemelach tochal* (*Avos* 6:4) that describes the various deprivations that one must endure in order to acquire Torah does not necessarily include eating out at restaurants or touring Eilat in a rent-a-car. If your child earns money during the summer, he or she can be expected to contribute to the costs. Similarly, even if your child's yeshiva or seminary does not have formal exams or other performance criteria, you can still set them up privately. For example, your son should present you with a study plan for the year, and if necessary, you can hire a *kollel yungerman* to test him on a regular basis. Parents who are paying for yeshiva have a right to monitor and measure their child's progress. Additionally, this is valuable training for when or if your child holds a job in the professional secular world. Everyone is accountable to someone. Why shouldn't a *yeshiva bochur* also be?

CONCLUDING THOUGHTS:

Though your child's newfound religious intensity may be disturbing to you, it is important to keep matters in perspective. Even if you assume that he or she is immature and misguided, which is not necessarily correct, becoming more religious is probably the mildest form of adolescent rebellion that today's parents face. After all, it could be worse. No one is using drugs or committing crimes. Many parents would envy you for this problem. So the best attitude to take is one of open-mindedness, patience, and understanding.

The Self

30

৵

Feelings Versus Actions: Torah and Psychological Perspectives

*B*ased on correctly and incorrectly understood psychological theories, many people have adopted the belief that it is healthy to express feelings and unhealthy to repress or try to control them. This viewpoint maintains that all feelings are OK, no matter how bad they may seem to be, and only actions are to be controlled. However, feelings do no harm and therefore should not be controlled.

The Torah seems to have a different view. Even the most cursory glance at the commandments indicates the Torah's compelling interest in us controlling our feelings. Examples of such are, the commandments to love your neighbor, not be jealous, not bear a grudge, and love God with all your heart. According to the Torah, it appears that some feelings, regardless of whether you act on them, are not OK.

In this chapter, we will explore the basis for the psychological belief in the importance of expressing feelings, and

discuss to what extent Torah philosophy supports or contra-
dicts this principle.

THE PSYCHOLOGICAL PERSPECTIVE:

In order to understand the basis for the importance some psychological theories place on feelings, you should be familiar
with the following assumptions that they operate under:

The mind can operate on many levels at the same time,
and an individual may only be partially aware of the reasons
for why he or she feels or acts in a certain way. A benign and
simple illustration of this principle in operation is when you
walk out the door and have a nagging feeling that something
is wrong. You stop and think for a while, and then are pretty
sure you forgot something, but cannot remember what it is.
It's "on the tip of your tongue." Then, you finally remember
what it is. How is it possible to realize that you forgot something, but not remember what it is? Either you remembered it
or you forgot it! Apparently, the mind can function on many
different levels of awareness. As you were walking out the door
and wondering about your day, another part of your mind was
reviewing what you had to do before leaving the house! In
other words, the unconscious mind may be thinking and feeling in ways that we are completely unaware of.

Parenthetically, the existence of the unconscious is merely
a theory. There is no empirical evidence proving its existence.
However, there are some interesting partial scientific proofs,
as well as some fascinating allusions to its existence in rabbinic literature. One such example, we find in regard to the
chief wine steward who "forgot" about Yosef. The verse states,
"And the chief wine steward did not remember Yosef, *and
he forgot him*" (Genesis 40:23). The *Ohr Hachaim* observes
(ibid., his first interpretation), that the wine steward did not
want to remember him; therefore he forgot him. (Also see
Rashi ibid., 41:12, which elaborates on the wine steward's

uncharitable attitude toward Yosef.) The implication being, though the wine steward "accidentally" forgot Yosef, he actually had a wish to forget him and removed him from his mind. In this example, the Torah seems to indicate that the human mind is under the influence of thoughts that operate on many different levels of awareness. This is strikingly similar to the concept of the unconscious mind. Nevertheless, whether the unconscious exists or not, the theoretical conceptualization of the unconscious mind and its associated mechanisms, has proven to be a useful tool for understanding mental processes and dynamics. This understanding has, in fact, led to effective treatments of various mental conditions.

In a similar fashion, there is an unconscious process regarding our fears, anxieties, conflicts, and other emotions. Unless we think about matters more deeply, we may be only partially aware of what is bothering us. It is theorized based on the above, that if one rejects or suppresses his feelings, at some point they will begin to exert an internal pressure as they become "bottled up." When you keep stuffing something into a bottle, the pressure builds, and at least one of three things will eventually occur:

1. As the pressure builds, it will progressively do damage to the "container." In this case, the container is the personality.
2. As the pressure builds, part of the contents might vent off and leak out suddenly and unexpectedly. In the case of a person's emotions, it might make him act on his feelings impulsively and without conscious forethought.
3. The container will explode and the contents eject themselves forcefully.

Obviously, these outcomes can be harmful, because then a person's actions are coming out of unconscious impulses or explosions, instead of rational planning and thought. For example, imagine a situation where you find yourself growing more and more annoyed at someone, but you never say anything about it to him. Then, one day, he makes a relatively small mistake and you blow up at him. He wonders, "What have I done to deserve this?" Later, you realize that you were angry about many other things, too. In this case, your anger all along was being repressed, perhaps because you felt that it was improper to be angry. Ultimately, you ended up acting in a far more unseemly and improper matter.

In the above illustration, the anger was not actually unconscious, rather it was semiconscious. However, there are feelings that are more deeply felt, more deeply repressed, and can ultimately cause much more serious damage to a person's inner life if not dealt with in an appropriate manner. For example, it is theorized that a person can suffer depression and lack of self-esteem when he feels intense unconscious anger and directs it inward. The person is afraid of the effects of, or feels guilty about, expressing his anger. Therefore, he unconsciously directs this destructive force into tearing himself apart. He is actually doing to himself what his anger would direct him to do to the other (i.e., "tear him apart").

To summarize, the psychological perspective on feelings is based on the idea that a person cannot completely control his feelings. What actually occurs is that the feelings are still felt unconsciously. If one continues to suppress them, it can be harmful because the stress is then felt inwardly, and will likely lead to acting impulsively as it bursts out in an uncontrolled manner. This is known in psychological terms as "acting out," because a person acts out an unconscious feeling.

THE TORAH PERSPECTIVE ON FEELINGS:

At first glance, the Torah expects us to control and suppress our feelings in many areas, especially in matters of the heart. As was stated earlier, there are biblical commandments to: "not bear a grudge" (Leviticus 19:18), "love your neighbor as yourself" (ibid, 19:17), and to "not hate your brother in your heart" (ibid). Is good Torah living and mental health incompatible? Not necessarily. A closer look at many of the prohibitions reveals a different picture.

For example, the Mechilta (Exodus 20:14) points out that the commandment forbidding one to covet the possessions of another is only violated when consummated with an action (i.e. theft or extortion). However, this still is not quite an endorsement for the psychological attitude that feelings and thoughts are not harmful, because the same Mechilta comments that the coveting will lead to sin.

An approach that seems to be very compatible with the psychological viewpoint can be found regarding the commandment to "love your neighbor" (Leviticus 19:17). Nachmanides notes the language of the verse in Leviticus is more correctly translated as "be loving *toward* your neighbor." He explains, though it is impossible to force yourself to feel love toward someone else, the Torah can command us to *act* in a loving manner. We see from this that the Torah does not always expect us to control and dictate our feelings.

Furthermore, a correct interpretation of the commandments to "not bear a grudge" and "to not hate your friend in your heart" actually shows the Torah's endorsement of the appropriate and respectful expression of feelings. The complete verse states: "Do not hate your friend in your heart [rather] rebuke him [for what he has done wrong]. And do not bear a sin on his behalf." The meaning of this is that you may not keep the hatred bottled up in your heart; rather, the Torah commands you to tell the person directly what he has done wrong to you. All this is so you won't come to hate him! (See Maimonides, *Yad, Deos* 6:6, and Nachmanides [ibid]) Obviously, your complaint should be stated in a respectful tone. This latter point is addressed by the end of the verse, ". . . and do not bear a sin on his behalf." Therefore, you are only prohibited to bear a grudge for the very reason that you should be speaking directly to the person about what he did wrong at the time the offense was committed. We can then say, the definition of "bearing a grudge" is to wait until the person needs a favor from you, and to only then tell him what you are upset about in a tit-for-tat fashion. But to discuss your resentment over what he did to you at a time prior to his request to borrow something, is not only permitted, but even expected!

Even with the above explanations, there are still many commandments that indicate the Torah's expectation that certain feelings be controlled and repressed. For example, "Do not follow after your eyes" (Deuteronomy 15:39), or "Do not be jealous" (Exodus 20:14). These verses clearly imply that certain thoughts are immoral, and the Torah prohibits people from thinking them.

Interestingly, regarding the prohibition of being jealous, Ibn Ezra (ibid) actually questions how it is possible to comply with this directive. He wonders how, if someone is really feeling jealous, it is possible to control one's thoughts and not be jealous! In order to answer his question Ibn Ezra reframes the issue. He points out that one cannot be jealous of a bird, because he knows that no one can grow wings and fly. Likewise, the Torah is asking us to be mindful of God's providence and to realize that all of our possessions are from him. Therefore, we have no cause to be jealous because we can only own what the heavenly decree allows us to own.

However, this Ibn Ezra is not in agreement with the psychological perspective. Whether his approach works or not, it still involves the suppression of feelings. Nevertheless, it is noteworthy that Ibn Ezra does acknowledge the difficulty and near impossibility of directly controlling a feeling. Instead of telling you to completely suppress the feeling, he proposes a way to circumvent it.

Are we then to conclude that the Torah does not see any harm in controlling and suppressing feelings? Is the psychologically postulated idea, that "bottling it up inside can be harmful," incompatible with the Torah view? Certainly, this would not be the first or last time that religious values did not agree with secular ideas. On the other hand, psychology aside, there is a compelling common-sense notion supporting the theory that if a person controls his feelings too much, it will be damaging. Many people have experienced this on a personal and firsthand basis. Furthermore, we saw before that a proper understanding of the commandment to "love your neighbor" and to "not bear a grudge" shows the Torah's clear endorsement of the healthy expression of feelings. So we then must wonder, is it that according to the Torah some feelings should be expressed and not suppressed, and for others, the opposite is true?

Perhaps we can understand the Torah's perspective on feelings in the following light. We all know the Torah prohibits eating certain foods because they are deemed to be unkosher. Even so, the Torah is not devaluing the role of eating in maintaining good health and bodily function. Similarly, we can say the Torah may prohibit certain feelings, but does not devalue the role of expressing feelings in the maintenance of a healthy mind and healthy interpersonal relationships. So in general, like eating, the expression of feelings is to be encouraged and performed regularly to maintain health. However, the Torah has isolated certain foods, as well as certain feelings, because they have been determined to be toxic to our spiritual health.

In conclusion, while there is some conflict between the secular idea that all feelings are OK, and the religious commandments proscribing certain thoughts deemed to be spiritually harmful, that is not the complete picture. On the whole, a careful examination of several commandments shows the Torah to be cognizant of the value of expressing feelings and the potential harm in the suppression of feelings.

31

❧

Guilt, *Teshuva,*
and Psychology

$\mathcal{S}$ome people believe, based on their understanding of psychology, that guilt, in and of itself, is unhealthy. Though psychology has identified certain kinds of chronic guilt to be stemming from pathological internal conflicts, that does not mean all guilt is unhealthy. Should we expect people to feel good about what they do wrong? Obviously not. Aside from psychological theory, common sense tells us that guilt is a useful emotion only if it spurs a person to correct his actions and change for the better. On the other hand, guilt is pathological if it paralyzes a person and causes him to give up hope. How does a person keep this feeling of guilt in a healthy balance? What does the Torah have to say about this?

From a Jewish philosophical perspective, a feeling of guilt is an important part of the *teshuva,* or penitence process. Rabbenu Yonah in the classic *mussar sefer, Shaarei Teshuva,* lists emotions such as regret, sorrow, fear of impending punishment, and shame as part of the requisite steps for achieving forgiveness. (See *Shaar Rishon, Shaarei Teshuva D'Rabbenu Yonah.*) Furthermore, we find in Psalms (51:5) Dovid *Hamelech* wracked with guilt: "My sins are constantly before me." *Chazal* learn from this that one must forever regret and feel bad about past sins, even years after repenting (*Shaarei Teshuva*, ibid). It would seem, as far as the Torah is concerned, a sinner should feel guilty even after he is presumably forgiven.

A PSYCHOLOGICAL PERSPECTIVE ON GUILT:

From a psychological perspective, guilt can be defined as an inner attack upon the self. For example, when a person feels that he has violated his morals, he feels guilty. Psychologically speaking, he is criticizing and condemning himself. There may also be an associated dread or fear of punishment. This experience can be understood as having a miniature parent or teacher inside the mind of a person, scolding him, and warning him to behave properly.

The psychological theory for how this inner "parent" develops is subject to many interpretations. However, one theory, in its essential form, is that the toddler undergoes a series of crises, resulting from a conflict between wanting to rebel and not listen to his parents, and wanting to please his parents and be loved by them. Additionally, the child may have resentment toward his parents for placing rules on him. He may be frightened by his own hostile impulses toward his parents, and in turn, the possibility of an aggressive reprisal. It is out of this crisis, and an effort to harmonize the conflicting parts of the personality, that a person's conscience is born. It is the job of the conscience to control this conflict in order that the child can still remain loved, and be protected from his own impulses and what they might bring.

Does this sound a bit farfetched? If you think about it, it is only logical that such a crisis and conflict should take place, as a child moves from the world of total self-gratification as an infant, into the world of reality where he also must please others in order to be loved. It is furthermore reasonable to assume that the child will have some resentment about these rules, and possibly a fear the resentment will lead to dangerous aggression on his part. The child then fears he will be a victim of similar aggression directed toward him. The tendency to see others' potential behavior in terms of one's own malignant intent, is known psychologically as "projection." The Talmud makes a similar observation about human nature when it states, *"Kol Haposel Bemumo Posel"* (*Kiddushin* 70a), which means that a person criticizes others with his own flaws. The child's personality must make order out of this conflict, and creates an inner "policeman" to control the peace.

People who criticize themselves too much, feel paralyzed by guilt, or are too ashamed of themselves to function with a reasonable level of self-confidence, may be suffering from an overactive conscience. There may have been circumstances that interfered with the normal development of the conscience, and helped create a less balanced internal structure. By the way, it is incorrect and an oversimplification to say that children whose parents were overly strict, will automatically develop an overactive conscience. This is because each child chooses to react differently, and may internalize his experience differently. The development of a personality is a far too complex and fluid process to attribute to any one particular matter. Sometimes, paradoxically, children who were underdisciplined have overactive consciences, stemming from an internal need to compensate. In such cases, through competent psychotherapy, a particular person's emotional difficulties can be explored within the light of past experiences and with the goal of changing underlying personality structures and defense mechanisms.

Knowing that some kinds of guilt can be counterproductive, it is most unusual and surprising that the major works on repentance by the early rabbinic authorities do not raise this as an important issue. Maimonides, *Rabbenu* Yonah, *Chovos Halevavos,* and *Mesilas Yesharim* all are completely silent. None of them caution against feeling "too guilty," "overdoing it," or "beating oneself up" in terms of guilt feelings. (Maimonides does warn against excessive fasting [Yad, Deos 3:1], but that is different than unhealthy guilt.)

Is this concept of unhealthy guilt just a modern excuse for lack of religious commitment? Perhaps the Torah perspective is that the more conflicted and anguished a person feels, the better off he is? In order to answer these questions, we must explore Torah and psychological perspectives on guilt in greater depth.

The *rishonim* did not place a limit on the extent of regret and anguish one should feel for having sinned. There are no cautionary words regarding feeling overly guilty. Yet, even if we put psychological theories aside, common sense and experience tells us there is validity to the concern that many people find guilt to be paralyzing and destructive.

In contradistinction to the *rishonim*, we find that the more contemporary *mussar* writings draw this distinction between constructive and destructive guilt. For example, Rabbi Zelig Pliskin's *Gateway to Happiness* devotes an entire chapter to guilt. He quotes liberally from *Sifrei Chassidus*, as well as the *Aley Shur*, about the dangers of pathological guilt.

What has happened here? How can we account for this difference between the earlier mussar writings and the modern ones? Is this yet another example of how we have grown weaker than the prior generations in our spiritual ability? Do we need someone to dilute the strictures of the Torah, in order to cater to our weaknesses? Not necessarily. The halacha has recognized that over centuries, even the biological realities and makeup of humans are subject to variations and change. (See for example, *Magen Avraham*, O.C., 179:8.) Certainly then, it is a reasonable conjecture that our cultural, social, and emotional realities, are also subject to variation from previous generations.

It may be that feeling regret, sorrow, or shame for one's actions, is an emotion of a different order than the self-critical, self-punishing internal experience we call "guilt." In fact, there is only one word in the Torah that is popularly translated as *guilt*. The word is *ashem*. However, *ashem* may be more accurately translated as *guilty of transgression*, as opposed to *feeling guilty*. (See Genesis 42:21 and Leviticus 4:13.) After clarifying our definitions, actually, there may be no conflict between psychology and the Torah regarding the appropriateness of guilt feelings.

Why is there no specific Torah word for feeling guilty? To some extent, the modern form of guilt is a luxury. When people have leisure, they have time to worry. This is more likely to occur when people have the basic needs of life already assured. Therefore, feeling tormented by guilt, becomes a term written about by people of the modern age. But for most of history, man was busier worrying about where his bread would come from, and was less focused on his internal states of conflict. As far as the *rishonim* were concerned, we can theorize that guilt was a more practical and focused experience. It involved feeling regret and shame for a committed transgression. Perhaps, they could not conceive of any rational person spending years and years in a paralyzed state of emotional conflict and turmoil, trying to repent and then feeling overwhelmed. However, modern man can relate to this all too well.

Interestingly, there may be a reference to this kind of conflictual guilt in Maimonides' "Letter on Religious Persecution" (*Iggeres Hashmad*). The goal of that treatise was to lend encouragement to those Jews who, under extreme duress, were forced to declare belief in Islam. Maimonides states that, according to Jewish law, they were obligated to face exile and expulsion instead of converting to Islam. Maimonides did not want those who remained and declared faith in Islam to feel utterly lost and in despair of ever returning to Judaism. He implied that it is acceptable to repent and return to observance of the laws in stages, and not to be overwhelmed by the multitude of sins that have already been committed. However, it is still significant that Maimonides did not mention this concept in any of his general halachic or philosophical writings. Perhaps from his perspective, it could only take an extraordinary and unusual circumstance, such as forced apostasy, to cause a person to be locked in a guilt conflict. Maimonides may not have seen a need to address the issue of unproductive guilt on a more general level, thus leaving it out of his *Laws of* Teshuva.

Fortunately or unfortunately, modern life presents new challenges. A person today can undergo years of emotional torture stemming solely from internal conflicts. This is an internal process that, to a large degree, people from less emotionally complicated societies may not have experienced. It is this modern state of anguish that the contemporary *mussar* authorities were cautioning against, not the feelings of remorse and regret that are a basic requirement of repentance.

CONCLUDING THOUGHTS:

Guilt can be a constructive or destructive force. It can compel a person to improve and develop his character, and in that context, regret and sorrow are natural and healthy. It is this process that the *gedolei mussar* were referring to. On the other hand, there seems to be a form of guilt that undermines a person's ability to work constructively. For reasons that we explored, there is little discussion about this from the early Jewish philosophical writings. Nevertheless, unhealthy guilt is addressed and cautioned against by later rabbinic authorities, perhaps due to particular social and psychological realities of the modern world.

If a person finds himself feeling paralyzed and overwhelmed by guilt, the goal should not be to learn how to simply "wipe away" the guilt and believe everything is fine. Rather, he should seek to address the underlying psychological issues that are causing this disproportionate guilt. This way, he can become free to respond to his guilt in a healthy and appropriate manner, and correct or change as his conscience dictates.

32

ॐ

Personal Autonomy and Kibbud Av v'Em

$\mathcal{A}$s therapists, we encounter many people who have conflictual relationships with their parents, or blame their current problems on their upbringing. Without passing judgment on the validity or appropriateness of such complaints, we have found that in order for some people to function better as a spouse or parent, it is often helpful to repair and improve their relationships with their parents.

As an adult, having a healthy relationship with your parents depends on many cultural, philosophical, psychological, moral, and religious factors. There are many viewpoints on this matter, of which not all of them are compatible with the halachic and traditional Jewish viewpoint. Nevertheless, regardless of the halacha and despite best intentions, we have found many observant people to be in varying degrees of avoidance, hostility, and conflict with their parents. Should they turn to strictly secular sources to resolve their problems, they might not be able to find suggestions that allow them to foster their mental health and be at peace with their religious values simultaneously.

In this chapter we will explore this issue from different perspectives, discuss their origins, the conflicts that they present, and hopefully offer some helpful guidance on how to utilize the best ideas from each of them.

THE MODERN SECULAR PERSPECTIVE:

Proponents of this viewpoint maintain that most people, upon reaching maturity, should seek to establish an "adult" relationship with their parents. They believe that as an adult, one is not necessarily bound to his parents in the same manner as a child. According to this secular perspective, adult children should act toward their parents as equals and treat them no more or less respectfully than they treat anyone else.

It is worthwhile to understand the origin of this value system in order to comprehend and grapple with its pervasive influence over our current thinking, whose source has its roots in America's unique place in world history. As a consequence of Western culture having recognized the significance of the individual and the value of personal autonomy, the democratic ideal is that each person has a right to self-determination. Americans feel that it is beneficial for a person to "strike out on his own" and try out new ideas and ways of living. Tradition is less important than innovation. This kind of thought process is inherent in most Americans by genetic and cultural tendencies. Almost everyone in this country either immigrated or descends from those who immigrated. In order to make and survive such a move, even if by necessity, such people were likely to have had a natural disposition to be able let go of the "old world" and live in the "new world." Ironically, it is this willingness to constantly challenge the old values that has been the source of this country's greatness as well as its moral lowpoints. If not for the openness of American society, previously oppressed minorities could never enjoy the kind of historically unprecedented freedom and tolerance of religion that they experience today. The absolute *brilliance* and almost prophetic insight of the founding fathers allowed them to create a constitution that would eventually cause the nation to free the very slaves they unwittingly and hypocritically did not consider to be equals. It's no wonder that Americans have a deep-rooted mistrust for authority. Not only did we free ourselves from the tyranny of our British overlords, but segments within our population used the very same principles to free themselves from their American counterparts. On the other hand, this lack of respect for tradition has led to an "anything goes" mentality, where moral atrocities are committed daily in the name of "personal freedom" and "choice." Similarly, the collapse of the family and erosion of the sanctity of marriage is also a by-product of this value system. Freedom for the individual above all else! Only in the past few years are people waking up to realize the emotional and psychic devastation that certain selfish lifestyle choices have left children with.

THE TORAH PERSPECTIVE:

The Torah is absolute in its requirement that children honor and respect their parents. The Talmud compares the honor due parents to the honor due to the Almighty. (See *Kiddushin* 31b.) The biblical commandments to honor (Exodus 20:12) and fear (Leviticus 19:13) one's parents are codified by the Talmud (ibid) as follows: What is the verse referring to when it says to fear ones parents? One should not stand in his place, sit in his place, contradict his statements, or "approve" his statements. (Note the high standard of respect. Even to agree with a parent is disrespectful, as it implies an unacceptable level of equality!) What is honor? One should serve his parents food and drink, help dress them, and escort them in and out of the house.

Furthermore, even when a person's parents are acting in a manner that is disrespectful and humiliating, which they are forbidden to do (see Maimonides, *Yad, Mamerim*, 6:8), a child is still not allowed to retaliate, or in any way return the disrespect. The Talmud is replete with stories where Jew, and even Gentile, suffered great humiliation at the hand of their parents, and still did not dishonor or disrespect them. (See ibid 31a. Also see Jerusalem Talmud, referenced by *Tosafos* "Rabbi Tarfon," ibid, 31b.) Therefore, even in cases where a parent is acting in an abusive manner, it is forbidden to retaliate. (Be advised: This chapter is written for adults looking to improve a dysfunctional relationship with their parents while remaining in harmony with Torah laws. If you are a child reading this, and your parents are being emotionally or physically abusive, do not try to get help from this column—share your problem immediately with a rabbi or teacher whom you trust!)

From a Torah perspective, it would seem that the age of the child is irrelevant. Even a fully mature adult must honor and respect his parents according to the biblical directive.

Some notable exceptions to this: A married man who hosts his father at his house, sits at the head of the table instead of his father. (See *Aruch Hashulchan* 240:11.) However, a close review of the context shows the source of the ruling is not based on any modern idea of adult autonomy; rather it is based on technical concerns for modesty vis-à-vis the daughter-in-law. Similarly, we find that a married woman is technically freed from the obligation to honor her parents when it comes in conflict with her ability to honor her husband (see Kiddushin, 30b). However, this does not give her any more autonomy than she had before, because she now is obligated to show similar respect toward her husband. For some, depending on how this is understood, a whole new autonomy conflict for women may be raised in regard to their obligations toward their husbands. Though a full discussion of modern versus traditional values in marriage is beyond the scope of this article, some of the conclusions and guidelines that we will draw may still be applicable.

THE DILEMMA:

Keeping in mind the strict requirements of honor and respect, is there any feasible psychological approach to resolving relationship problems with your parents? In order to properly follow the commandment, must one simply learn to tolerate and overlook any real or imagined hurtful parental remarks or behavior? In other words, is it possible, within halachic guidelines, to resolve relationship problems with parents by sharing constructive criticism? Or is that a secular idea, and halachically speaking, there is no choice but to, out of respect, tolerate and overlook any hurtful remarks or behavior from parents?

We believe there is a way to enter into a constructive and corrective dialogue with your parents while remaining within the parameters of respect. Pragmatically speaking, and even from a Torah perspective, given the average person's inability to absorb abuse without retaliating, it is optimal to try to change a hostile or hurtful parent's behavior. This is because, the best-case alternative for most people in such a situation, would be to avoid and distance themselves from their parents. This, too, falls short of giving parents the honor they deserve. (Parenthetically, this is a course of action allowed by halacha under certain extreme circumstances. See Maimonides, *Yad, Mamerim*, 6:10, and *Aruch Hashulchan* 240:16.)

PSYCHOLOGICAL CONSIDERATIONS:

Our approach will require that you be careful and exacting in what you say and how you say it. If you have a long and complicated history of difficulty with your parents, it will be hard to keep within the guidelines without letting your temper flare up. Therefore, before we delineate our guidelines and rules for this approach, it is helpful to have a better understanding of some of the possible psychological dynamics behind adult parent-child conflicts.

Often, hostilities and resentment mask deeper unresolved dependency issues. For example, Malka might resent greatly certain comments or criticisms that her mother makes, or that she never praises her. However, the level and degree to which it hurts and angers her is more a function of her own insecurity than any meanness from her mother. The stronger the feelings of resentment, the stronger the unconscious need for attachment. This causes her to "go looking for trouble" as she self-consciously seeks approval when she is almost sure that her mother will be critical or unsupportive. The results are predictably hurtful. That is not to say it wouldn't be better if a mother was less critical, only that it is important to see the matter more objectively. Once you are able to do this, you are in a better position, emotionally, to improve your interactions.

WHAT TO SAY:

Keep in mind, while according to the halacha, it is disrespectful to tell your parents that they are wrong, there is nothing disrespectful in letting them know how their actions make you feel.

Sample Statements:

"When you say that, it makes me feel small."
"Ouch, that really hurts my feelings."
"I am very sad that you don't seem to be happy with me/ what I am doing."

How to Say it:

1. Make sure you have a clear understanding of the halachic requirements and restrictions regarding honoring your parents.
2. Always stay calm and speak in a respectful tone.

3. Make no judgments, criticisms, or suggestions about whether your parent has done anything wrong. Instead, inform of him how it made you feel. Try to use passive feelings such as, hurt, sad, and ashamed, instead of aggressive feelings such as, angry, mad, disgusted.
4. Be careful, as not every statement beginning with the words "I feel" are feelings. If you say, for example, "I feel you are being unfair, mean, and so forth," such statements are judgments and criticisms, not feelings.
5. In order to have the most impact, it is best to state your feelings immediately when you are being hurt. (Of course, if you are too upset to speak calmly, it's better to wait.)

It may sound simple, but if you consistently and persistently let someone know when he is hurting you, he will eventually stop. Be patient and repeat this procedure, over months if need be, and as many times as it takes. Eventually, almost everyone will achieve results with this method. In addition, you will find that this method can be used in all relationships as a way to help someone change while avoiding major confrontation.

33

❧

The Stigma
of Psychotherapy

𝓕or many people, particularly certain segments of the Orthodox community, going for psychotherapy treatment is seen
as a last resort. There appears to be a strong stigma associated with mental-health counseling. We have encountered
many cases where people have suffered needlessly because
they avoided and delayed treatment until their situation was
desperate.

Even now, as current events regarding "children and adolescents at risk" have been publicized, psychotherapeutic
treatment is seen as an emergency response to a crisis. In
addition, it would seem that the rallying cry of "let's protect
our children!" is needed as an added reinforcement, or even
excuse, for seeking counseling. But why is this necessary?
Why shouldn't people suffering from problems in living feel
free and uninhibited to try a form of treatment that many
find to be helpful? It is not as if Orthodox Jews avoid anything other than traditional medicine. Exotic herbs and vita-

mins, hypnosis, biofeedback, and chiropractic are all treatment options exercised freely without the degree and hesi-
tancy associated with psychotherapy. (Please note: We are
neither endorsing nor critiquing these treatments. We are
merely noting that though these treatments have been rejected by certain circles of traditional medical thought, they
still have many adherents within the Orthodox community.)
What is the cause for these apparently strong and negative
associations within our culture? In this chapter, we will attempt to understand and explain the psychological and sociological bases for this stigma.

A PARADOX:

Many physicians have reported from their experience that the
Orthodox Jewish community is generally more scrupulous
about personal health than the average population. Perhaps
this greater consciousness regarding health matters can be at-
tributed to the Torah's ethical directive to preserve one's health
(see Maimonides, *Yad, Deos* 4:1). Having observed this phenomenon, it is then even more perplexing why engaging in
preserving mental health has been viewed so negatively by this
same community.

Some might say the atheistic and heretical views of Sigmund
Freud have contributed to the religious community's anath-
ema toward psychotherapy; however, that alone does not
provide an adequate explanation. After all, the entire discipline of medicine is based on a general scientific approach as
well as the specific biological sciences, with many major discoveries made by those who espouse secular and irreligious
views such as the theory of evolution. Even so, we have never
seen a Jewish religious person refuse a state-of-the-art medical treatment because it was discovered by an atheistic scientist! In addition, we personally have found rabbis of all sects
of Orthodoxy, to be strongly in favor of psychotherapy treat-

ment to their constituents when needed. Therefore, there must be another basis for the extreme shame and embarrassment that some people report experiencing when it comes to seeking mental-health treatment.

A MORAL INDICTMENT:

When someone needs medical help or suffers from a physical disease, this condition is not viewed as coming out of any personal or moral deficit. It appears that people generally see their Torah observance, or failures in observance, as not being directly responsible or related to their health. People consider it a natural part of life to occasionally become ill, and at times, to need medical treatment.

However, psychological health seems to have a stronger connection in people's minds to spiritual well being. Our perception is that many people seem to feel if one follows the Torah way of life, they should not suffer from depression, anxiety, and dysfunctional relationships. For example, some may see their compulsive anxiety and fears as a sign that they do not have enough *bitachon* (faith in God). Or perhaps they consider their marital or familial difficulties as stemming from poor *middos* (character traits). Taking this into account, the very need for psychotherapy or marriage counseling may be viewed by some to be an indictment of their moral character.

Interestingly, the Jewish philosophical view on health and medical treatment is not so clear-cut as the popular sentiment. Nachmanides states, "When God is pleased with the actions of a man, he has no need for doctors." Nachmanides's view is that a righteous person, who is on the highest spiritual level, should only seek a cure for his illness through repentance and prayer. (See his commentary on Leviticus 26:11. Please note that Nachmanides is discussing a theoretical religious ideal, specifically referring to the era of the prophets when people would go to the prophet to pray for their cure. Do not attempt this today for obvious reasons.) On the other hand, Maimonides disagrees with this philosophy, and considers the need for medical treatment to be as natural as the need for food. Prayer should be an augment to medicine, but never a substitute. There is a tradition that a "book of cures," written by King Solomon, was deliberately hidden by King Chiskiya because people were relying on the cures themselves instead of prayer. Maimonides rejects this story on the basis of his philosophy that there is no moral weakness in seeking medical cures. Therefore, he concludes that this tradition is contrary to common sense, and if this book existed as described, the righteous King Chiskiya could not possibly have done such a thing. (See his Commentary on Mishna, *Pesachim* 4:10.)

Nevertheless, regardless of whether it makes sense from an accurate understanding of Jewish Philosophy, people tend to see mental illness as a sign of moral failure, and physical illness as just bad luck. Perhaps this is a part of why religious people feel shame for needing psychotherapy.

A THREAT TO THE TORAH?

Another contributing factor in the stigmatization of psychotherapy, is its power to affect people's behavior and character. If, after seeking treatment, a person is able to function better in his relationships or is less anxious, it might be considered a threat to the primacy of Torah. Could therapy be more helpful than studying *mussar*? If a therapist helped cure someone from his anger, one might ask, "Why was his rabbi or rebbe unable to do so?" Worse yet, what if a nonreligious or non-Jewish therapist, as a result of the emotionally curative power of therapy, helped a patient to improve his character traits? Was the divine Torah somehow proven to be deficient? (See Maimonides, *Yad, Deos,* 2:1, who clearly advocates seeking rabbinic counsel for "illnesses of the soul."

This would seem to lend support to this argument. However, in support of the idea that one can heal "illnesses of the soul" through non-Torah sources, we find Maimonides, in his introduction to his commentary on Mishna *Avos*, raising no objection to using appropriate secular sources as an aid in moral character development. In fact, he informs the reader that he deliberately did not mention the names of the sources that he quotes, out of fear that some readers will automatically reject them because they are not Jewish.)

In response to this imagined threat to the authority and curative powers of the Torah, a more balanced outlook is required. Though people can indeed benefit greatly from the moral guidance that the Torah so richly provides, the Torah as we are capable of understanding it, may not necessarily provide us with access to all the psychological and developmental remedies that it takes for a particular individual to achieve mental health. (Compare this to Nachmanides's statement: "The Torah does not have its civil laws rely on mircales." See his commentary on Leviticus 26:11.) A wise person once said, "Our rabbis were among the greatest of psychologists." A wiser person added, "And you need to be a great psychologist to understand our rabbis."

CONCLUDING THOUGHTS:

Many people are needlessly ashamed of mental illness and emotional difficulties, and seem to feel that their problems are as a result of inferior moral character. In addition, people may fear seeing a psychotherapist because they believe that somehow, all the answers to life's problems should be found in Torah and mussar. While there may be some aspects of these objections that deserve consideration, in most instances, they appear to be misunderstood and misapplied. If you were considering psychotherapy but felt ashamed or afraid, we hope that this chapter helps clarify some of your conflicts and concerns and helps you see them in a new perspective.

A LETTER AND A RESPONSE:

After a series of our articles on this subject appeared in the *Jewish Press,* someone wrote to us with a question and comment. This person's remarks as well as our response is below:

Dear Rabbi Simcha and Chaya Feuerman, CSWs:

Although I agree that the atheistic and heretical view of Sigmund Freud are not necessarily the only reasons for, as you say, "The religious community's distrust of psychotherapy," I do believe that it may still play a role. Psychotherapy is different from other medical services that a person may use. The personal and moral views of a scientist do not affect the treatment. Presumably, a newly discovered medical treatment would be implemented identically whether the scientist is a religious person or an atheist. However, if a person is using a therapist who incorporates Freud's views into his work, it may have a detrimental effect on the religious observance of a person insofar as the treatment may incorporate values that are against the Torah. For example, my understanding is that Freud held that religion was neurotic and pathological. Therefore, there would be some reason for a religious Jew to avoid seeing a therapist that has such views.

Our Response:

In your letter you made an excellent point regarding how the personal and religious values of a practitioner of psychotherapy can potentially be more damaging than the values of any other medical practitioner.

Your points are certainly valid; however, we ask you to consider that while your point is technically valid, on a practical level the opposite may be true. Your observation assumes that a patient has a deep and influential relationship with a psychotherapist, but in regard to a practitioner of other medical services, the patient is just a receiver of the medical treatment. For example, a doctor prescribes medication or exercise, while a psychotherapist will tell a patient how to handle his relationships. But is this really so? We submit that most people experience a deep sense of trust when they speak to and relate to their doctors. Thus, the morals and religious orientation of any medical practitioner can be highly influential. To illustrate, a religious woman may take advice from her gynecologist regarding halachic aspects of family planning along with medical advice, or parenting advice from a pediatrician that has relevance to halachic issues. (In fact, sometimes the practitioners who claim to be religious or knowledgeable about religion can be even more dangerous in this regard, because the patient's guard is lowered and she is more trusting and suggestible when a so-called religious doctor gives her halachic advice.)

In addition, there are often intense emotions flowing back and forth between the patient and the healer, such as, the patient's feelings of dependency and the practitioner's need to respond in a paternal or maternal manner. Because of this, many practitioners are induced to respond to these feelings inappropriately. In fact, there is a study that showed that doctors tend to give overly optimistic prognoses for terminally ill patients. While the doctors may be trying to respond out of compassion, psychoanalytically speaking, they also may be defending themselves against facing these painful feelings of mortality. No one likes to be reminded about death, and doctors may not welcome the feeling of helplessness when they cannot "make it all better." This can be damaging, because a person in such a situation, if requesting a truthful and complete answer, needs to have a clear idea of what to expect in order to plan his remaining days.

Since psychotherapists utilize, study, and interpret the dynamics of the therapeutic relationship as the very means for promoting healing and growth (clinically known as "the transference," which was "discovered" by Freud and which he wrote about extensively) they actually may be the least likely to abuse their influence over the patient. As we have mentioned in prior articles, most theories of practice require a psychotherapist to remain neutral and objective and to avoid imposing his or her beliefs on the patient. The key issue is that no matter what kind of medical professional a person consults with, one should look for an individual who understands the boundaries and scope of his practice and is self-aware enough so that he will not trespass over them.

CHAPTER

34

❧

The Psychological Aspects
of Questions of Faith

$\mathcal{M}$ost people consider questions of faith to be primarily a religious matter. People experiencing doubts struggle to accept certain beliefs and alternate between feeling guilty, ashamed, angry, and rebellious. Some may turn to rabbis, friends, and teachers for guidance. Others will try to wrestle with the problem intellectually by studying various philosophical and religious works.

One aspect of this difficulty that is hardly ever explored, is the emotional component. While there clearly is value in trying to grapple intellectually with crises of faith, this may not hold the key to resolving doubt. (As to the relative merits of simple faith versus using scientific proofs to support it, see the introduction to the *Lev Tov* edition of the *Chovos Halevavos*.) In this article, our goal is not to answer or solve any questions. Instead, our goal is to bring another dimension of inquiry into the process, in order to assist a person who is conflicted about his or her religious beliefs.

A THOUGHT EXPERIMENT:

Most people would like to think of themselves as rational beings, who make decisions based on logical thought and learned experiences. However, there is evidence to the contrary. In fact, there have been fascinating studies on the nature of decision making that show that many, seemingly rational decisions, are emotionally driven. Try this out on a couple of friends. Ask some of them scenario #1 below, and some of them scenario #2.

Scenario #1:

"You are a commander of an elite rescue squad. Your mission is to rescue sixty hostages. If you attempt a rescue, there is a 98% chance that twenty people will be *killed*. If you try to negotiate, the odds are unknown. Do you rescue or negotiate?"

Scenario #2:

"You are a commander of an elite rescue squad. Your mission is to rescue sixty hostages. If you attempt a rescue, there is a 98% chance that forty people will be *saved*. If you try to negotiate, the odds are unknown. Do you rescue or negotiate?"

If you try this experiment, you will likely discover that most people who are asked Scenario #1 will vote for negotiation, and most people who are asked Scenario #2 will vote for a rescue mission.

Guess what? Believe it or not, what was described in both scenarios are identical! (Go ahead, reread the questions carefully and you will see!) Generally, you will find that people who are asked Scenario #1 will be more hesitant to vote for a rescue because their question emphasizes the twenty people who would die if they did so. On the other hand, Scenario #2 emphasizes the fact that if they elect for a rescue mission, forty people will surely be saved.

This thought experiment shows how so-called rational decisions are influenced greatly by emotional considerations. In this case, the desire to *save* a portion of the hostages versus the dread of killing a portion of the hostages becomes the major influences in the decision-making process. Keep in mind, if you were to ask the ones who made the decision, they would likely give all kinds of rational, moral, and strategic reasons for their choice. However, at the root of it all, it may be an emotional response and not a rational one.

In this same light, when people have doubts in their faith, a hidden factor may be the emotional issues involved. If the emotional issues are resolved, the burning nature of the questions will often be mitigated.

GETTING TO THE HEART OF THE MATTER:

If you, or someone you know, is experiencing doubts or conflicts about religion, an honest answer to the following simple question will reveal any hidden emotional issues: "Why now?" Why is this question an issue now? After all, whatever question or doubt this person is having surely could have been asked before. The response is the clue to the emotions that lie hidden beneath this question of faith.

For example, a young person might say that he began to have doubts about religion as he became more independent from his parents. In trying to resolve these doubts, it is important to consider the emotional process this young man is engaged in. As part of his effort to become an adult, he is reconsidering the values that he was taught as a child. For this person it may be necessary to feel that he has chosen his faith, *independently,* rather than blindly following what he was taught. Of course, his parents and community hope that he will come to accept these values as his own, and if his experiences growing up were mostly positive, it is likely that he will. If he, or those who he trusts, do not respect his emotional need for independence, the difficulties will be exacerbated.

By the way, much of the concern parents have with children "going off the *derech*" (the path of Judaism) can be addressed by working on strengthening the parent and family relationships. To illustrate, imagine a young person who feels close to all his family members and feels comfortable in his community. Even if such a person has doubts about religion, he would be crazy to alienate himself from those who he loves and respects. At worst, he would remain a closet and quiet disbeliever. This alone ought to be sufficient emotional glue to keep him religious, and tide him over during the stormy and destabilizing stage of adolescence. Once he matures, he will be more likely to remain religious because he will have enough positive experiences to convince him of the benefits of this lifestyle.

As another example, a person who has doubts about God's providence may have just experienced some kind of sudden change in his life circumstances whereby he no longer feels sure or confident that he is being taken care of. What really is troubling this person is that he suddenly feels all alone in this world.

CONCLUDING THOUGHTS:

A person who is struggling with doubts about religion may attempt to "talk it into himself," or ask others to provide him with convincing proofs. People in this situation feel tormented and conflicted. Though it may be helpful to explore these questions and doubts in an intellectual and rational manner, it is also helpful to put questions such as these within their proper emotional and psychological perspective. Nearly all doubts, or difficulties in observance, manifest themselves at particular times because of various circumstances in a person's life. If these emotional issues are addressed adequately, oftentimes, the questions and doubts become less significant and easier to understand.

35

ᢒᡝ

Can Psychotherapy Be Self-Administered?

Someone asked us, "Assuming a person studies different psychological theories, is it possible to give himself psychotherapy?" This question, we suspect, lurks in the minds of many of our readers. Though people are not usually tempted to treat their own medical problems, there does seem to be a desire to self-treat psychological problems and avoid seeing a therapist, perhaps due to the private and personal nature of mental-health difficulties. The volumes of psychology self-help literature written in the last twenty years are ample testimony to this fact.

In order to answer this question properly, it is necessary to have some sense of how psychotherapy works and what kinds of conditions it treats, as some problems may lend themselves more easily to self-diagnosis and treatment than others. Without describing in-depth the various psychological theories and treatments, we will discuss some of the basic assumptions and principles that many theories and forms of treatment have in common.

THEORETICAL ORIGINS:

Many psychological theories, in some manner or form, postulate that the human mind is multifaceted. Meaning, a person may not be completely aware of all that he is thinking or why he does what he does, and in fact, may have constructed various rationalizations and behaviors as adaptations to his circumstances. As often is the case in adaptations, they serve a purpose at the time, but may continue to be in effect long past the period of their usefulness. These adaptations that were once helpful, at a later time, may be dysfunctional. The mind is unable to disengage from this dysfunctional adaptation without some help. This is because the adaptations were adopted as a defensive measure against a perceived threat to the ongoing functioning of the personality. To illustrate, someone from an abusive home may have learned to keep his feelings bottled up and not to talk back. For most children, a certain amount of complaining and testing of the rules is a normal part of healthy development. However, for this child, the repercussions of normal childish disobedience were too severe. Therefore, this child learned to be meek and unassertive as a method of protecting himself from abuse. Later in life, this person may still have difficulty asserting himself. Since people many times will have a negative reaction to someone who asserts his opinion, the behavior remains self-reinforcing. This person will avoid confrontation out of fear of having an argument or "making waves." What he does not know is that he is no longer a child and he need not be so fearful of an occasional negative or hostile response. After all, in the course of human affairs, all people get into arguments. Unfortunately, this person remains locked in the past, and emotionally only has a child's tolerance for disagreement. Thus, he will remain passive and avoidant of confrontation.

The example above is just one possible explanation for the origin of this problem; in fact, there are many psychological causes for passivity and unassertiveness. But for the purpose of this illustration, let us assume this is the psychological root for his unassertiveness. The question then is, can a person with enough knowledge of psychological theory identify the origins of his problem? Furthermore, even if he manages to *identify* the problem, he still has not solved the problem. This is because to solve the problem, the person will have to do more than learn a new behavior. This problem has strong roots in this person's emotional life. He may intellectually acknowledge that his fear of confrontation is irrational, but feeling ready to overcome this fear requires psychological maturation and development. That is not something that self-insight alone will automatically generate. Both of these tasks, identifying underlying maladaptive psychological defenses, and working to develop the necessary capacities to function freely without them, are extremely difficult to perform on yourself. It takes a considerable amount of objectivity to see yourself clearly as you really are, and to then have the courage to change. Even with the help of a therapist, this is no easy task.

Because a psychotherapist is trained to remain objective, for this reason alone he can be extremely helpful in solving psychological problems. By remaining objective, a therapist can see things that the patient is blind to. But that is not the only reason why a therapist is able to help people solve problems. A psychotherapist relies on interpersonal techniques and interventions that allow him to more easily identify and remedy psychological difficulties. Psychotherapy is a process where psychological defenses and adaptations are uncovered, analyzed, and replaced with more functional thoughts and behaviors.

HOW PSYCHOTHERAPY WORKS:

The properly trained psychotherapist, can:

1. Recognize some of the common kinds of defense mechanisms and how they typically lead to dysfunction.

2. Remain neutral and objective without letting his or her emotions interfere and cloud judgment. A therapist also can provide the person in treatment with neutral and objective feedback about current functioning or dysfunctioning, without complicating the emotional climate with demands and/or criticisms as family and friends often inadvertently do. As we shall see in our example below, this skill is critical. Frequently, a person's defenses will arouse many negative emotions in others, making it extremely difficult to do or say anything helpful. By remaining detached and neutral, but still fully aware of his feelings and the patients' feelings, the therapist enters into a special kind of relationship with the person seeking help. Over time, this relationship can become what's clinically known as a "corrective experience." This may be the only relationship where he receives clear, direct, but nonjudgmental feedback about how he relates to others. This is particularly important when the patient is seeking treatment for interpersonal difficulties.

The process of psychotherapy allows a person to gradually become aware of some of his defenses, and to reevaluate the necessity of their existence. This is *not* chiefly a cognitive process; instead, it is principally an *emotional* one. A person can let go of his old adaptations only if he is comfortable enough and ready to make a change. These concepts may be better understood by way of example:

Case Scenario:

Michael has a bad temper. Recently he almost lost his job because he shouted at his boss. His wife is fed up and concerned about the children. Michael is a caring husband and father, but just cannot seem to get his anger under control. He has tried learning *mussar*, has spoken to his rabbi, and has made resolutions, all to no avail.

To understand Michael as a therapist might, it is important to keep in mind that all human behavior can be seen as rational and purposeful. Even the most malignant personality traits can be seen as having once been a constructive effort to cope with a given set of life circumstances. Remember though, what is constructive and adaptive behavior for a child, may not be functional or useful for an adult. Unfortunately, *many emotional responses know no age.* If Michael chose to see a therapist for this problem, the therapist might speculate to himself as follows: How was this anger once functional for Michael? The therapist would then work with Michael to uncover why he is convinced that this behavior is still helpful and beneficial. Michael may not be aware of, or in touch with, his unconscious feelings about the benefits of this behavior.

It could be that he was overindulged as a child and was able to get what he wanted whenever he wanted by having a tantrum, so he persists in doing so based on an underlying conviction that he will continue to get what he wants. Or, perhaps, he was exposed to a lot of anger as a child, and actually remains terrified and insecure. He compensates for his terror by terrifying others, thereby giving himself the comforting illusion of being in control. In reality, the possibilities are endless. Only by working with the therapist over time, can this tangled emotional issue be unraveled. Once it is unraveled, it still may take time for Michael to become emotionally strong enough to overcome his original fears, or develop the capacity to delay gratification. Once again, it is through the therapeutic relationship that this is best achieved.

At this point, it becomes clearer why, in most cases, self-therapy is extremely unlikely to be effective. Even if a person can somehow see his behavior objectively enough to uncover his past adaptations and defenses, he must also have the emotional strength to confront whatever fear prompted his adaptation and let go of it. Nevertheless, having said that, there are certain kinds of treatment that a person may be able to self-administer. Those treatments are the kind that focus on cognitive or behavioral interventions. These therapies help people change their way of thinking, manner of communication, and responses to anxiety, based on new learned experiences. An example of this is the different kinds of interpersonal, family, and marital interventions that have been suggested in our other essays. However, even those treatments are much more effective when administered by a trained therapist, since it is much easier to change behavior within the neutral but supportive context of the psychotherapy relationship. Many behaviors have a psychological origin in the past, and therefore may resist all efforts toward change without it being fully understood and emotionally accepted via a therapeutic process.

CONCLUDING THOUGHTS:

It is extremely unlikely for a person to successfully self-treat moderate to severe mental-health conditions, due to the emotionally interactive nature of psychotherapy treatment. On the other hand, if a person feels that he just needs a few pointers or suggestions on how to cope with interpersonal issues or mild anxiety, he may be able to benefit from certain cognitive or behavioral interventions that are found in self-help books.

36

☙

The Psychological Dynamics of the *Shaala* (Halachic Question)

*H*alachic questions play a major role in an Orthodox person's life. Highly intimate matters, regarded by the secular world as completely in the realm of "personal freedom and choice," are routinely decided and ruled on by rabbinic authorities. Though the issues may seem to be largely procedural and legalistic, in fact, halachic questions often involve hidden, complex, and conflicting emotions. In this article we will explore some of the psychological dynamics of a *shaala*, and how they impact upon the questioner's ability to articulate, comprehend, and follow the halachic ruling.

AVOIDANCE BEHAVIOR:

We have found that many people delay or avoid asking halachic questions. They will endure years of vague guilt or unnecessary stringencies, instead of simply clarifying their question. Some may be afraid of hearing the answer, because they do not wish to comply. However, avoidance is not the psychologically healthy approach to most matters. An emotionally mature person is able to face reality head-on. If the answers pose problems or challenges, they should be worked out and dealt with. This is true from both a religious and psychological perspective.

Interestingly, in some cases, there is a halachic concept that it is preferable to let someone sin out of ignorance of the law, if you know he would sin even if he was informed that it is forbidden (see Talmud *Shabbos* 148b). Even so, to remain willfully ignorant is to remain stagnant. The road to growth clearly lies in bracing yourself to confront your obligations.

We have also found that some people, men in particular, will avoid asking halachic questions because they loathe to humble themselves and be at the mercy of someone else's expertise. (Anyone who has driven around with a man for hours, who refuses to roll down the window and ask directions, has witnessed this phenomenon firsthand!)

Sometimes, a person will go ahead and ask a *shaala*, but leave out vital information. Since many halachic questions are of a highly personal nature, the asker may be tempted to understate his need. He may feel embarrassed about his need for a *kula* (leniency). This is unfortunate, because many halachic rulings are dependent upon life circumstances. Factors such as financial loss, *sholom bayis* (family harmony), and mental health can indeed be a consideration. The rabbi cannot function as a mind reader, and he can only base his ruling on the facts that are given. (See Talmud *Bava Basra* 131a, "The judge can only rule by what his eyes see.")

PATHOLOGICAL DOUBT:

As we mentioned above, halachic rulings are often dependent on particular circumstances. Most people trust in the expertise of the rabbi, and assume that he will clarify important details. Unfortunately, some people, when receiving a lenient ruling, may develop doubts later on. They might think, "Did I really understand him correctly? Did I overstate or understate a particular point? Maybe I really am *not* allowed to do such and such. . . ." If this occurs once in a while, perhaps this person is just being careful and conscientious. However, if it occurs regularly, and similar doubts are present in other areas of his life, it is likely part of a larger syndrome. This syndrome is clinically known as Obsessive Compulsive Disorder. One of the symptoms of OCD is constant checking behavior or repetitive behaviors (e.g., hand washing, repetitive ordering or organizing, and checking.) OCD is a difficult condition to treat, and psychiatric as well as psychotherapeutic intervention is required.

THE "TRICK" QUESTION:

The Midrash has recognized that people can use and abuse halachic questions to promote a hidden agenda. See for example, Rashi Genesis 25:27, where Esav misleadingly asks Yitzchok if one must tithe salt, in order to appear conscientious.

One should be careful to avoid using halachic questions and answers inappropriately as leverage in interpersonal arguments. For example, someone who is involved in a family conflict or power struggle about whose *minhag* (custom) to follow, may ask a rabbi, "What is the proper custom for some aspect of kiddush or the Pesach Seder." The question may be valid, but the asker is withholding a major part of the story. The rabbi, unwittingly, is being used to take sides in an argument. "See, even rabbi so and so agrees with me!" In addition to the procedural question, it would be constructive to address the emotional issues by trying to peacefully resolve the familial conflict.

CONCLUDING THOUGHTS:

Because halacha and its rituals pervade all aspects of the Orthodox Jew's life, the act of asking a halachic question can be
affected by a person's psychological makeup. Some people
may allow various emotional issues to disrupt clear communication between themselves and the rabbinic authority, inadvertently leading to distortions. Self-awareness of the possible
psychological pitfalls will enhance the experience of asking a
shaala, and help maximize spiritual growth and well being.

37

✌

When You Get the "Blues"

Generally, you are an optimistic and confident person. However, today you are feeling run-down and irritable. You are ready to snap at your spouse or children for the most minor infraction. What happened to change your mood, and is there anything that can be done about it? In this article, we will not be discussing clinical depression, which is a serious mental-health condition that requires treatment. Rather, we will be discussing a transient and passing bad mood, or the "blues," that otherwise healthy and functioning people experience from time to time.

You may be wondering, if this condition is transient and not serious, why discuss it at all? The answer is, in learning how to handle such moods, you can decrease their severity and duration. In addition, as you shall see later on in this chapter, often these moods come as a reaction to deeply held personal assumptions. Once these assumptions are better understood and examined rationally, you will be able to strengthen your character, and it will open doors for you to become more confident and successful in many situations.

THE ORIGIN OF THE "BLUES:"

It is important to realize that though this mood will probably pass on its own accord, it is *not* a random occurrence. With some effort and introspection, you can trace its origins. Usually, this kind of mood comes from either a comment or experience that deflated your ego or crushed your self-esteem.

Many times, after thinking about it for a bit, you will immediately discover what it was that upset you. Sometimes though, it will be more difficult to put your finger on exactly what circumstance brought about this emotional state. If you are unable to recall a precipitating event, try to remember when you first started feeling this way. Then, try to recall if anything unusual or disturbing occurred around that time. Once you have identified the experience that seems to have put you in this bad mood, ask yourself what exactly was hurtful to you about what occurred or about what was said. For example, you may have made an error at work. Actually, the mistake happened several weeks ago, but today your boss spoke to you about it. For some reason, you seem to be so bothered by what occurred that it has spoiled your mood for the next few hours, or even days. Why has it affected you so? It is significant that when you discovered the error you were not so upset. You became upset only *after* your boss spoke to you. If you search carefully, you will discover that there is some basic assumption about your self-esteem or your capabilities that has been threatened, challenged, or in some way damaged, by this event. Perhaps you have always prided yourself on your superior performance at work. If you were to look a little deeper, you may discover that this assumption is actually a defense against more disturbing thoughts. When the assumption is threatened or challenged, the disturbing thoughts assert their dominance and become manifested in your bad mood. What are these disturbing thoughts? Perhaps you are not satisfied with your career or job choice? You may have been telling yourself, "Well, I don't really like my job, and/or it is not the most fulfilling experience, but at least I am good at it!" When your boss delivers the criticism to you, your rationalization is temporarily disrupted, thereby putting you in touch with your general feelings of dissatisfaction with your career. This may not be something you are ready to deal with because it presents too many challenges and uncertainties, so you repress this thought and just end up feeling vaguely irritable and dissatisfied.

There are some precipitating events that are not based upon what others have said or done to you, but instead they are based on certain events that occurred and how you choose to internalize them. For example, you scratched your car while parking, or received a parking ticket for an expired meter. Or you just bought something and realized that you forgot to use the coupon and could have saved twenty dollars. In these examples, though many people would be disturbed about this kind of thing, many would not. After all, the monetary value may be relatively insignificant to your total budget. What assumptions are at work here? Perhaps you feel that you must not make "stupid mistakes." When you discover that you have made what you consider to be a "stupid mistake," a wave of self-criticism washes over you. People who have little tolerance for their own mistakes may be masking their own fear of the many unknown and uncontrollable tragedies that can occur at any time. The need for control and perfection regarding life's hassles and occasional setbacks is a way of maintaining an illusion that one can be protected from the more serious and tragic accidents. At the moment the minor mishap or "stupid mistake" occurs, this rationalization is challenged. Consider this: If you could dent your car, you could also be in a fatal car accident. Not everyone is able to stay emotionally in touch with this; so instead, some may unconsciously bolster the unrealistic notion that they can be perfect and avoid all mistakes. Of course, these are just examples of the many possible unconscious dynamics to serve as an illustration. It will take careful thought and analysis for you to uncover what is really bothering you.

WHAT TO DO ABOUT IT:

Now that you have elevated your thinking to a more sophisticated and insightful awareness of your emotional processes, your underlying assumptions can be brought out into the light of day and evaluated rationally. In the example of the error made at work, perhaps you need to face the reality that you are unsatisfied with your job. Having accepted this consciously, and difficult as it may be to do, you can begin to take the steps necessary to change your situation. In the "stupid mistake" example, you should assess to what extent you were being careless and to what extent you were a victim of circumstances beyond your control. For the former you need to address your behavior, for the latter you need to develop a greater emotional tolerance of uncertainty and loss.

CONCLUDING THOUGHTS:

As with many psychological insights, being intellectually aware of an aspect of your personality or behavior alone does not produce change. Your bad mood is not going to just evaporate in the face of this analysis. A process of personal development is required over a long term, and that only comes with time and experience. Nevertheless, understanding yourself and what is really upsetting you is the first step.

38

❧

A Midrashic Metaphor on Mental Illness

*T*he *Yalkut Shimoni* (131) relates a story about how King David questioned the purpose of insanity. (Presumably, David only asked about mental illness because other forms of illness could be understood, since they humble a person or cause him to repent. But a person who is insane is unable to reflect on his condition.) It is obvious from many of the psalms the extent to which King David was a great observer and admirer of the wonders of God's creations. However, according to this Midrash, King David saw no purpose for insanity, and therefore questioned why God would have made insanity part of the human experience. God answers David, "You will one day see firsthand what insanity is for." The Midrash reports that later on in David's life, while running away from Saul, he is forced to seek refuge at the palace of the king of the Philistines. The guards recognized him to be the one who killed Goliath and wanted to kill David out of revenge. In order to avoid this fate, David feigns insanity. Ultimately, the king of the Philistines dismisses him as a harmless lunatic and releases David unhurt. The Midrash seems to be implying that King David learned from this experience that insanity has a purpose in allowing him to escape.

This Midrash is difficult to comprehend. Are we to accept that the suffering of all the hundreds of thousands of individuals throughout time who were afflicted with insanity is somehow justified by it once having saved King David's life? Could there not have been other ways for him to be miraculously saved? True, there is a concept in Jewish philosophy that entire world events can be providentially arranged for the sake of one solitary righteous God-fearing individual. To illustrate this, Maimonides, in his introduction to his commentary on the Mishnah, gives an example of a palace having been erected that remained standing for years, solely so that a tzaddik could take shelter in it for one day many years later. Even if the intention of this particular Midrash was to teach this point, it still then has not really answered King David's basic question. King David was rightfully questioning the *function* of insanity, which is different than finding out how it may incidentally be of help to someone. For example, one might wonder what the *function* of bees is in the ecosystem. If he was told that they pollinate the flowers, thereby helping them reproduce, that is a valid explanation of the bees' function in the animal kingdom. On the other hand, if he is told that one day the bees would swarm to protect a certain tzaddik, though that also may be true, it still does not explain the bees' *function* and therefore does not answer the question.

THE METAPHOR BEHIND THE MIDRASH:

In order to make sense of this, a deeper understanding of this Midrash is required. The Ramchal (author of the *Mesilas Yesharim*) in his introduction to *Aggada* (printed in the first volume of the Midrash *Rabbah*) states that some *Aggados* and Midrashim may use metaphors to explain ideas and concepts that the rabbis did not wish to relate openly. Furthermore, he is of the opinion that the metaphoric stories or descriptions themselves do not have to make sense, because they are in service of a deeper meaning below the surface. Along these lines, we would like to suggest that *Chazal*, by way of this Midrashic metaphor, are offering an insightful explanation and interpretation of the function of many kinds of mental disorders.

It has been observed that often so-called "crazy" behavior is actually a sane and adaptive response to crazy circumstances. Extreme examples of this can be found in documented studies of survivors of the Pol Pot regime who developed hysterical blindness in response to visually traumatic events. Nothing could be found medically wrong with their sense of sight; nevertheless, they remained "blind." Presumably, the sights they saw were so horrifying that one part of their mind was actually able to shut off access to eyesight as a defense against the overwhelming and terrifying visions. This can be compared to a circuit breaker that shuts off the electricity when the wires get too hot, in order to avoid a fire.

Though the above example is extreme, there are also examples of the functionality of mental disturbances that arise in everyday life. For example, consider the case of Shalom, who underperforms and misbehaves in school. Everyone is baffled because he is apparently very intelligent and has not shown any major learning disabilities. We have previously elaborated on the concept of the basic human drive for competence. It is then doubly hard to imagine why Shalom would deliberately sabotage his success. In cases such as this, sometimes an underlying unconscious individual and family dynamic may be the cause. And in fact, Shalom's behavior may be rooted in a misapplied attempt at function and competence. Let us suppose that Shalom has many other siblings, all of whom are brilliant, talented, and successful. Due to the interplay of many factors including disposition and temperament, learned behaviors and experiences, and environment, Shalom has made the unconscious decision that he cannot compete with his sibling's performance. In order to protect himself from the feelings of failure, and also the despair of losing attention, he decided to take a different route. Shalom decided to "succeed" at failure. This accomplishes two goals for Shalom. First, he can always tell himself that he really could succeed and be competent, he is just *choosing* not to do so. This can be compared to opting for an incomplete on your transcript instead of risking failing the course. So Shalom has opted to take an "incomplete" on the course of life. Second, Shalom may in fact receive more love and attention by "failing" than by "succeeding." This is because Shalom indeed may not be as brilliant as his siblings are, and would never be able to compete in the same arena.

Returning to our Midrash, *Chazal* may have been trying to illustrate this basic observation by way of King David's story. Namely, mental illness and insanity can be viewed as an adaptive response to extreme circumstances. David's behavior was perfectly sane for the "insane" circumstances he found himself to be in. He also was able to employ his mental dysfunction as a defense. Likewise, many people may paradoxically learn to "fail" as a way to "succeed" as in our above example. In addition, many other personality disorders and disturbances can be better understood and seen from this perspective.

A WORD OF WARNING:

The purpose of this article is, by way of a possible interpretation of a Midrash, to lend credence to, and educate people about, one theory of origin for some emotional problems and mental disorders. As we have pointed out in previous articles, understanding a possible psychological cause for a problem does not mean that it is easily solved. All of these "decisions" that we have discussed are unconscious and not ordinarily accessible to the person who has made them. Please do not accuse or blame a person who you believe is exhibiting such behavior. Even if you confront the person directly, he will be likely to deny it. However, certain methods of psychotherapy employ techniques that allow an individual, or even a family, to become more cognizant of unconscious dynamics. Once the individual or family is psychologically and developmentally ready to face and accept the unconscious material, other more functional and adaptive responses can be integrated into the individual or family personality.

39

❧

The Psychological
Meaning of Boredom

*I*n this chapter, we will discuss the psychological meaning of boredom and teach you how to listen to the special and personal message that your boredom contains. If you apply some of the principles in this article, the times that you consider the most boring and unproductive can become special opportunities to learn and grow.

Most people assume that the cause of boredom is from not having anything interesting to do. For example, a person who is bored may be unemployed, underemployed, not challenged in his current occupation, or lacking in a fulfilling relationship of family and friends. This is largely a mistaken notion. People confuse not having anything to do with being bored, while in fact, one does not necessarily cause the other. Though having something productive to occupy yourself obviously minimizes your experience of boredom, boredom, in and of itself, is a separate emotional state arising from particular psychological factors. Not having anything to do really means that you have nothing to distract you from whatever else you might be feeling.

Paradoxically, the people who claim that they never experience or are never bothered by being bored, in fact may be the most susceptible to boredom. Such people are adept at keeping themselves always very busy, and are able to occupy themselves almost all the time. They do this in order to avoid boredom. However, should they find themselves in a situation where they cannot keep busy, such as being stuck on a long line at the supermarket or sitting through a long-winded speech, they become extremely uncomfortable.

WHAT BOREDOM REALLY MEANS:

Psychologically speaking, one can say that there really is no such thing as boredom. Some psychological theories define boredom as occurring when a person is unable to distract himself from an uncomfortable feeling. The particular feeling varies based on the person and situation. When the feeling is unbearable, as a defense, a person will get restless and bored. Does this seem strange or farfetched to you? Think about it some more. When a person is bored, he really is unable to tolerate being alone with himself. What is this so-called bored person in touch with that he *so much needs* to be distracted from?

A THOUGHT EXPERIMENT:

The next time that you find yourself bored, try to sit quietly and discover what you are really feeling. Are you anxious or guilty about something? Are you mad at someone? This may take a little practice to train yourself to think in this way, but it will yield significant discoveries. This is because if you become aware of what is making you feel uncomfortable, you will have a chance to address personal issues that you may have been avoiding dealing with. While you are waiting around doing "nothing" you can use the time well to think about your life.

THE MESSAGE BEHIND BOREDOM:

People who fall asleep during the rabbi's speech, or people who claim that they talk in shul because they are bored, might be doing so for deeper reasons. Perhaps, on the surface, the rabbi's speech is boring, but could it also be that the listener is being forced to confront something about himself that he is afraid to face? Similarly, is the long davening and *hosafos* during *krias hatorah* (weekly Torah portion) really boring, or is the contemplative silence and the attendant emotions that being in the presence of God arouses, too much to bear without retreating into childish babble? Who knows what we would have to change about ourselves, if we even acknowledged for one whole minute *"Lifnei Mi Atah Omed"* ("Before whom we are standing"), during the typical two-hour-long *Shabbos* davening?

CHILDREN AND BOREDOM:

Some parents live in terror of the rainy-afternoon wail, "Mommy, I'm bored and have nothing to dooooo!" You cannot very well expect children to meditate on the meaning and purpose of their lives while they are bored. Nevertheless, the psychology of boredom in children is essentially the same as adults. The only difference is the application of age-appropriate techniques.

Children have the most difficulty with boredom because they are not yet as proficient in regulating their internal states. They fidget and complain not because they are bored, but because they are uncomfortable for one reason or another and have not devised a way to distract themselves. As with any developmental task, parents should be supportive and sympathetic but not overly involved. Parents should communicate in a firm but empathetic manner their expectation that their children learn how to occupy themselves. For example, a parent might say, "You feel like there is nothing to play with this afternoon; that can be hard for you. But if you keep thinking, I'm sure you can come up with something." As long as you supply your child with a reasonable and age-appropriate selection of toys, games, and activities you need not feel guilty—no matter how much whining you hear. If you make it clear that your child's boredom is not your problem, but rather his developmental challenge, over time you will hear fewer and fewer complaints.

CONCLUDING REMARKS:

It is not boredom, per se, that people who have nothing to do suffer from. Rather, it is the semiconscious feelings that well up in our minds when we have no distractions. During idle time, we become more aware of unpleasant thoughts and dissatisfactions that we have been pushing away and avoiding. However, avoidance is no way to grow emotionally. Instead, during this "down time" of our lives, we can try to accept, address, and plan steps to change what we are unhappy about.

40

⤳

A *Kollel* Survival Guide

$\mathcal{T}$he areas of religion and money, each by themselves are often a major focus of marital and familial discord. The *kollel* experience, which involves an intersection of the two, is potentially fraught with emotional and interpersonal conflict. In this chapter, we will discuss some of the psychological issues that confront couples and families who are in *kollel*. Our goal is neither to support nor criticize the social and religious practice of the *kollel* experience; rather it is to help young couples make an informed choice, by providing them with objective information.

BACKGROUND:

For the purposes of this article, we define *kollel* as the practice of Jewish religious married men committing most or all of their day to studying Torah as a long-term career. Many people find happiness and fulfillment in such a lifestyle, and grow to become moral and spiritual models for their communities. Participants in *kollel* understand that they are living a religious ideal. They are willing to suffer deprivation in order to attain a high level of Torah scholarship, thereby benefiting the Jewish community at large, as well as leading a more spiritual life.

However, as in all life choices, there are always those who are not completely happy with their choice and encounter various unanticipated difficulties. Most *kollels* provide little or extremely modest stipends, so a person in *kollel* must somehow manage to financially support himself and his family. This is frequently accomplished through a combination of four methods below:

1. Parental/In-law support.
2. Wife working.
3. Government programs (HUD, Food Stamps, Medicaid).
4. Savings prior to marriage and wedding gifts.

DEPENDENCE BREEDS HOSTILITY:

To the extent that any system relies on an outsider is the extent that it is vulnerable to unwanted influences or controls. When a person feels controlled, aggression is an automatic psychological response. If a couple is having difficulty managing their relationship with their parents or in-laws, being financially dependent on them will only exacerbate the situation. As a preventative step, before entering into a *kollel* arrangement dependent on parental financial support, a mature, frank, and open-ended discussion should take place between all parties. Though many people find it difficult and even consider it rude to speak directly about money, if this is not done, the potential exists for serious misunderstandings. As it says in the Talmud, "There is no *kesuba* (marriage contract) without a [financial] argument." (See *Shabbos* 130a, and *Tosafos*, *Kesubos* 2a, *"Layom"*.) The tone for this discussion should be as neutral as possible, with an emphasis on thoroughly exploring all the philosophies and opinions of the parties involved in a nonjudgmental matter.

Once the opinions are stated, a pragmatic and practical understanding can be arrived at that is based on the available resources, without necessarily condemning any particular viewpoint.

We have encountered cases where parents and children widely diverged on exactly what the *kollel* arrangement would entail. For example, a parent may be under the impression that his child and child-in-law would be in *kollel* for a "year or two," and then embark on a secular career. The couple may be expecting that they would be financially supported for as long as necessary. Both parties might have unconsciously avoided clarifying this issue in advance for fear of seeming petty and "ruining the *shidduch*." In reality, the *shidduch* problems will only be more intense two years later.

KOLLEL AND THE "AMERICAN WAY," OR WANTING TO "HAVE IT ALL:"

Today's modern American lifestyle of leisure and plenty can make it difficult for young people to realistically assess and prepare themselves for financial deprivation. It is not unusual to see a nineteen-year old *yeshiva bochur* pulling up to his day of Torah study in a late-model car fully wired up with high-tech telecommunications and audio equipment. Although his dad may find the cellphone, stereo, and car expenses to be minimal based on his financial realities, all these "necessities" of modern life are difficult to maintain on the income that a *kollel* couple can usually earn.

- When the young couple was courting, of course they went to all the nice restaurants in the city. After they got married, they still may feel a "need" to celebrate every now and then, but how does that fit into their budget? It may prove to be hard for them to change their standard of living.

- The *kallah* was outfitted with a first class trousseau and selection of custom *sheitels*. Who pays for replacing these items when they inevitably get worn-out?

While parents/in-laws may have agreed to support the couple, and husband and wife may have agreed to live modestly and spend conservatively, there may be a wide divergence in opinion between exactly what are deemed to be "necessities."

KOLLEL AND THE NEED TO FEEL COMPETENT:

In other chapters, we have discussed the basic human drive to be competent. Whether you are an infant learning to grasp and crawl, or an adult striving to learn a profession, succeeding at your task brings you great pleasure. One of the challenges of the *kollel* experience is attaining a sense of mastery and competence in an area as vast as Talmud and halacha. Though many can become a master electrician, an expert lawyer, or a medical specialist, few who study Gemara can claim to have full mastery over the vast sea of halachic and Talmudic writings. A person may have learned and accomplished a great deal in Torah study, but aside from the titles of "rebbi," "rabbi,"and "*rosh yeshiva*," there are few external signs of this achievement. In some ways, it can be compared to an accomplished concert pianist or violinist who still must practice several hours a day in order to attain a level of perfection that few people can even properly critique. At least the musician gets to perform in front of a large crowd, but the "Talmud virtuoso" performs in virtual solitude.

Of course, the Torah viewpoint is that a person should study Torah for its own sake, and should not be concerned with personal status or prestige. Furthermore, regarding the study of Torah, we are all familiar with the dictum from *Pirkei Avos*, "It is not upon you to finish the work, but neither are you free to absent yourself from it" (2:21). Nevertheless, that having been said, most people still need to feel like they are accomplishing something concrete. From a spiritual point of view, the person studying Torah may be constructing entire *olamos* (spiritual worlds or creations), but in day-to-day life it may not feel that way.

In order to combat this, some *kollel* learners will set goals for themselves. A common choice is to study for semicha (rabbinical ordination), but there are also other goals that are less dependent on the particular yeshiva's curriculum or policy. For example, one might work to complete certain *mesechtos*, compile *chiddushei* Torah into a printed *kuntros*, or even submit voluntarily to a *bechina* (examination). These strategies certainly make sense from a psychological perspective.

LEAVING *KOLLEL*:

As the financial demands of a growing family increase, many must consider leaving *kollel*. Though often those who have spent many years in *kollel* choose professions closely related to Torah study, or professions that allow them to continue to dedicate a significant amount of free time to the study of Torah, many still feel uneasy with the decision.

As therapists, our role is not to grant moral absolution to people. So if a person feels that he has somehow failed in his moral duty, it is not our place to confirm or deny this. However, we do have an observation about the process of leaving *kollel* that can hopefully forestall unnecessary or excessive guilt by helping people realize a potential no-win situation: No matter how long someone stays in *kollel*, whenever he decides to leave, he is particularly vulnerable to feeling like a failure. This is because there is no fixed amount or time limit on how many years a person should be in *kollel*, so a person will only leave when his tolerance and abilities are exhausted. So whether he quits after one year or ten, he is quitting not because he has finished or completed something, but rather because he or his family cannot manage any longer. It is important to see one's leaving *kollel* in an honest, but also realistic, manner.

AVOIDANCE BEHAVIORS:

Of course, people can distort and misuse any mitzvah or ritual, and a *kollel* person is not exempt from this. Some people believe that *kollel* is a way to avoid the financial responsibilities of the "real world," and criticize *kollel* people as being unrealistic and unfair to their communities and families. Once again, we are not taking sides on this matter in a general sense. However, it is indeed possible that a particular person who harbors immature ideas about the nature of his responsibilities and has not made adequate career plans, might "hide out" in *kollel* as a way to avoid facing the intellectual and emotional challenges of the work world. Since this is a personality issue, such a person would probably show a history of avoidance behaviors not just limited to this sphere. For example, he may have always avoided performance challenges even in his Jewish studies in school, or he may neglect his responsibilities regarding parenting and maintaining his household. However, this is not the only judgment one can make, as this system has proven itself to be viable over the years, and in its own way, extremely productive. Certainly, if you suspect a loved one of engaging in such behavior, proceed with extreme caution when confronting him.

CONCLUDING THOUGHTS:

The social and religious institution of *kollel* is an accepted way of life for many religious people. Being in some way separate from society at large makes unique demands on the individuals and families of its participants. These demands may include adjusting to a different set of financial realities than one's family of origin, as well as being able to feel competent and productive with less tangible and concrete goals than the secular professions. Without entering into the debate that some might have in favor of, or against this lifestyle, we have sought to provide an overview of some of the psychological and emotional dynamics that *kollel* couples and families may experience, and how to best handle them.

41

❧

Accidents, Torah, and Psychology

$\mathcal{F}$or the most part, both Torah philosophy and many psychological theories maintain that there is no such thing as an accident. At the very least, both systems of thought do not take accidents for granted as merely uncontrolled and unplanned events. Rather, they should be investigated for any possible underlying cause. Though the Torah's basis for this view and psychology's basis for this view originates from different philosophical perspectives, they are not necessarily mutually exclusive. In fact, an awareness of both perspectives can enhance self-awareness and personal growth. In this essay, we shall discuss in detail the psychological and spiritual meanings of accidents.

A TORAH PERSPECTIVE ON ACCIDENTS:

As you may already know, the Jewish philosophical viewpoint is that there is no such thing as an accident. This is true both in regard to what happens to a person, and what a person himself does. For example, in Exodus (21:13) regarding someone who accidentally kills someone, it states "And God caused his hand." How is God "causing" this accident, and why? Rashi (ibid) explains that the victim actually was someone who committed murder at a prior time and evaded punishment. The accidental perpetrator was someone who committed accidental murder at a prior time, and also evaded his appropriate punishment (exile). So God causes these two fellows to cross paths, and the murderer passes underneath the ladder, while the "accidental murderer" falls off the ladder and kills the murderer. What apparently was an accident, according to the Torah, is in fact, divine retribution. In the final reckoning, both people received the fate they deserved. The purposeful murderer is killed, and since this event occurs in front of witnesses this time around, the "accidental murderer" must face his punishment and go into exile. Lest you might think that there is divine intervention only on major issues such as punishing murderers, the Talmud implies that even the inconvenience of pulling out the wrong change from your purse is a punishment.

(See Erchin 16b. Note this Gemara's stance strongly suggests that the *Chazal* believe even momentary and insignificant occurrences to be providential in nature. Although, strictly speaking, one can interpret this Gemara as merely advising that one should *experience* even a small moment of suffering to be for the purpose of atonement, regardless of its actual origin. In other words, suffering accepted with a proper attitude automatically expiates the sin, even if it is not a divine punishment. A full discussion of the Torah's view on providence (*hashgacha pratis*) is beyond the scope of this essay; however, we can safely infer from the above references that according to the Torah, an event that appears to be entirely accidental is not to be automatically viewed as such. This stems from a religious belief in the active involvement and intervention of God in earthly affairs.)

Seeing the emphasis placed on divine providence, one might be tempted to minimize the role that man himself plays in the determination of his fate. However, that could not be farther from the truth. Even King Pharaoh was held responsible for his actions, despite God attesting that he will harden his heart and that Pharaoh will refuse to let the Jewish people go. (For a detailed discussion of this, see Maimonides, *Shemona Perakim*, Chapter Seven. Also see Nachmanides and *Seforno*, Exodus 7:3.) Furthermore, a man is even held responsible for an accidental sin, such as when he forgets a particular law or rule. (See *Daas Zekainim Mebaaley Hatosafos*, Leviticus 4:2.) As we have quoted earlier in this book, a scriptural example of personal accountability is found in regard to the chief wine steward who "forgot" about Yosef. The verse states, "And the chief wine steward did not remember Yosef, *and he forgot him*" (Genesis 40:23). The *Ohr Hachaim* observes (ibid, his first interpretation) that the wine steward did not *want* to remember him; therefore he forgot him. (Also see Rashi ibid, 41:12, which elaborates on the wine steward's uncharitable attitude toward Yosef.) The implication being, though the wine steward "accidentally forgot" Yosef, he actually had a wish to forget him and removed him from his mind. In this example, the Torah seems to indicate that the human mind is under the influence of thoughts that operate on many different levels of awareness. This is strikingly similar to the concept of the unconscious mind that we will discuss in the next section.

A PSYCHOLOGICAL PERSPECTIVE ON ACCIDENTS:

According to psychoanalytic theory, man is a conflicted being. Beneath the surface of his refined and mature personality exists a veritable tempest of primitive thoughts and emotions such as jealousy, greed, anger, and lust, to name a few. According to this theory, although we are largely unaware of these intense unconscious thoughts and feelings, they still may be a strong influence on our behavior. Our conscious mind represses these thoughts due to their unacceptability and threat to daily functioning, yet they may still "leak out" by causing us to act them out.

For example, when a person comes late for an important meeting, is it an accident? He may claim that he left his house on time and it was not his fault that there was traffic and so forth, but did he leave himself enough time for contingencies? If not, given the importance of the meeting, why not? If it is a person who is chronically late, there may be underlying psychological causes. This person, despite many efforts to change his personality may be unable to do so because he is acting out unconscious feelings that are exerting even greater pressure on his behavior than his conscious wish to be on time. He may feel anger or resentment toward those he feels seek to control him, and therefore fights this control by coming late. Or perhaps he has a need to be noticed and get attention by being the last person to walk in the room. Or, perhaps on the few occasions that he makes it on time, he gets rewarded with a feeling of superior mastery and success as he "beats all the odds." Whatever the case may be, as a rule of thumb, if a person finds himself unable to change particular traits in his character, psychoanalytic theory will attribute it to an unconscious wish exerting force in the opposite direction. Some forms of psychotherapy use special techniques to help a person uncover these unconscious wishes and conflicts in order to allow the conscious mind to exert more control. This particular psychological theory ascribes to the idea that the unconscious mind exists. Though there is no unequivocal proof for the existence of the unconscious, there are compelling reasons for postulating its existence, as we shall see in later on.

To illustrate how and why according to this theory, our minds develop this mechanism of repressing undesirable thoughts and feelings, let's use a thought experiment. We may assume by observation that infants originally have only impulses and a need to gratify them, without any moral thoughts or a conscience. Gradually, via various developmental experiences, the infant/child's personality begins to coalesce and grow. This overlay sorts out and processes the various impulses and drives, and acts as a policeman and control mechanism. When an infant is hungry he will cry until he gets fed. When an adult is hungry, he will remain aware of his driving hunger but also plan out how he will obtain his food. Under severe emotional stress, a personality may crumble and temporarily return to its original state. For example, a person who has gone without food for days may be reduced to whimpering and crying "ma ma." Imagine a young infant who is in an absolute rage at his mother for not giving him the food he wants at the time that he wants. Perhaps he wants a spoonful of oatmeal cereal instead of formula. He does not yet have the vocabulary to address his needs, so he has very few communication options other than a cry of frustration. He feels rage for not being understood, and perhaps an urge to be aggressive, but then he may acknowledge that if he retaliates against his mother he will be helpless, and certainly won't get any food. So, he represses his rage in order to survive, and literally "swallows his anger." Erik H. Erikson, in his seminal work *Childhood and Society*, speaks of this regarding an infant who must learn to curtail the pleasure he experiences in biting down in order to nurse from his mother without causing her to withdraw. (This gives a new layer of meaning to the phrase "biting the hand that feeds you!") Thus to some extent, our very survival is dependent on being able to repress feelings.

Of course, like many adaptations that we make to survive, what was once the best choice may no longer be so helpful in our current situation. Returning to the example of the person who is chronically late, if he is acting out unconscious resentment at those he feels are controlling him, this is a pattern of relating that he may have learned to use early in life. We can hypothesize that as a child, when he felt excessively controlled, there were few options available other than to act out his resentment by passive resistance, such as, indirectly delaying and avoiding complying with requests. Even if the child had the verbal skills to express himself and indicate how he would like to be treated, perhaps in his family he would not have found a receptive audience. Instead, he chose to repress his resentment. However, to this day, this resentment continues to express itself through chronic lateness. This person will have great difficulty overcoming his lateness unless he can understand and learn to appropriately channel his need to passively flout authority.

SYNTHESIS:

As we stated in the opening of this chapter, the Torah and psychological viewpoints we have described are not necessarily mutually exclusive. As we discussed earlier, despite the Torah doctrine of divine providence (*hashgacha pratis*), there is an equally strong emphasis on personal accountability. The psychological approach that we have described offers a highly sophisticated perspective on personal accountability. Not only must we be aware of our conscious thoughts, but we also can strive to develop a greater understanding of our unconscious motives and drives.

A person who wishes to employ a dual Torah and psychological perspective, might employ the following model for responding to personal mistakes and accidents:

When an accident or mishap occurs:

1. Try to ascertain if there was any way to avoid it.
2. Try to understand what possible conscious or unconscious motivations may have contributed to the occurrence. Then find a more constructive way of expressing these feelings (e.g., mature discussion and problem solving).

3. If the accident caused you some pain or misfortune, the religious perspective requires that you search your actions for any sins that might have brought this punishment upon you. (See Talmud *Berachos*, 5a.)

4. In addition, if the accident involved a sin *b'shogeg* (resulting from forgetting a Torah law), the religious perspective would require you to improve your knowledge of the Torah to avoid a reoccurrence.

AFTERWORD

We hope that you have found these essays to be informative and helpful. Should you have any questions or comments, feel free to contact us in care of the publisher or via email at simcha-chaya@excite.com.

We also are working on a new book that will focus on self-discovered solutions individuals, couples, and families have used to overcome difficulties in their lives. If you feel you have some wisdom and experience that you would like to share, you can contact us to arrange for an *anonymous* interview.

Index

ABOUT THE AUTHORS

Rabbi Simcha Feuerman, CSW, and Chaya Feuerman, CSW, maintain a private practice in Queens, NY. They specialize in treating families and couples as well as work with individuals who experience religious conflicts. In addition to their private practice, the Feuermans author a weekly column on religion, relationships, and ethics for *The Jewish Press*.

Chaya Feuerman received her master's degree in social work from Adelphi University. Prior to entering private practice, she has held clinical positions at the Bleuer Psychotherapy Center in Forest Hills, NY and Pesach Tikvah Outpatient Mental Health Center in Brooklyn, NY. Chaya has also received post graduate training in psychodynamic therapy at the Bleuer Center and in Systems Family Therapy at the Minuchin Center for the Family.

Rabbi Simcha Feuerman has received rabbinical ordination from Yeshivas Ohr Hachaim, in Queens, NY, as well as Rabbi Meir Gruenberg Z'tl ("The Kayzmacher Rav"). He received a master's degree from Touro College in Medieval Jewish History and a master's degree in social work from Yeshiva University's Wurzweiler School of Social Work. In prior positions, Rabbi Feuerman has served as a pulpit rabbi at the Young Israel of Massapequa, Long Island, and a clinical social worker for the Jewish Child Care Association and the Long Island Consultation Center. He received post graduate training from the Philadelphia Child Guidance Center. He currently serves as the Pastoral Advisor for the Hospital for Joint Diseases Ethics Committee. Rabbi Feuerman is also the author of *The Family Sefer Hachinuch* (Jason Aronson Inc.).